The Magic of Christmas

LEISURE ARTS, INC.
Maumelle, Arkansas

Table of Contents

Santa Tissue Box Cover....4
Reindeer Tissue Box Cover....8
Sleigh Table Decoration....12
Reindeer & Santa Ornaments....22
North Pole Lineup....26
Snow Family Lineup....36
Reindeer Kiss....46
Santa Kiss....47
Candy Cane Climbers....48
Holiday Magnets....56
General Instructions....60

Santa Tissue Box Cover

Design by MizFitz.

Size

6 3/4"w x 9 1/4"h x 5"d
(fits a 4 1/4"w x 5 1/4"h x 4 1/4"d boutique tissue box)

Supplies

Three 10 1/2" x 13 1/2" sheets of 7 mesh plastic canvas
Worsted weight yarn
#16 tapestry needle
Two 12mm wiggle eyes
1/2" pink pom-pom
1/4" white pom-pom
Craft glue

Stitches Used

Alternating Scotch Stitch, French Knot, Gobelin Stitch, Overcast Stitch, and Tent Stitch

Instructions

Follow charts to cut and stitch Santa Tissue Box Cover Pieces. Use matching color Overcast Stitches for all joining unless otherwise noted.

Join Sides along long edges. Matching ★'s, join Hat Front to Front and Sides, stitching through three layers of canvas. Use white Overcast Stitches to continue joining Front to Sides.

Matching ✖'s, tack Beard to Front. Tack Mustache and Eyebrows to Front. Glue eyes and pink pom-pom to Front. Join Top to Front and Sides.

Matching ▲'s, join Hat Top to Top. Tack bottom edge (ball area) of Hat Top to Beard.

Join Star pieces along unworked edges. Tack to Hat Top.

For Bird, tack Beak and Wings to Bird pieces; join along unworked edges. Using red Overcast Stitches, join Hat pieces along unworked edges. Place Hat on Bird. Tack Feet to Bird. Tack Feet to Top. Glue white pom-pom to Hat.

Color Key

white	rose
peach	red

Front (30 x 38 threads)

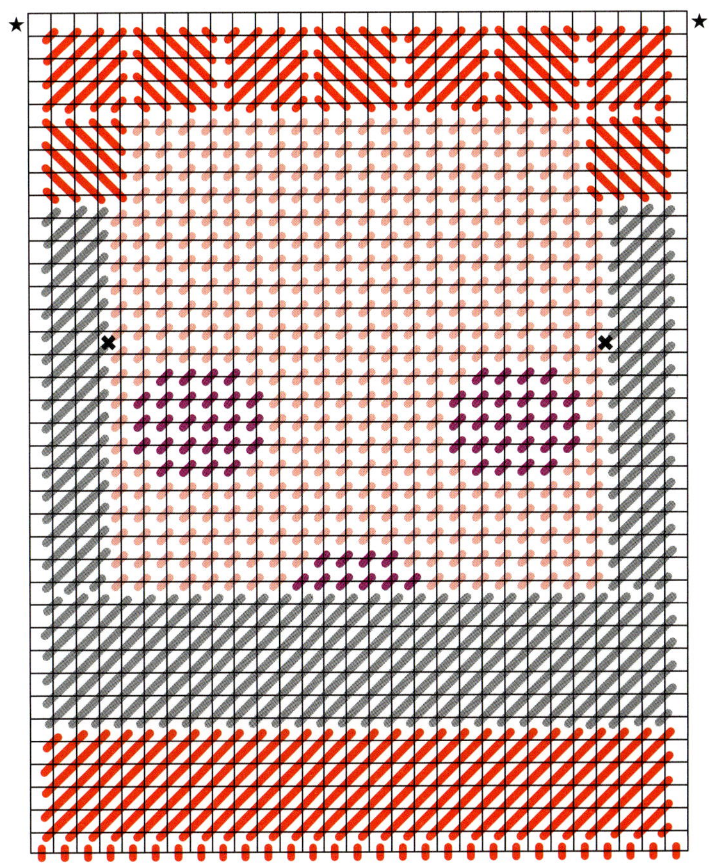

Side (30 x 38 threads) (stitch 3)

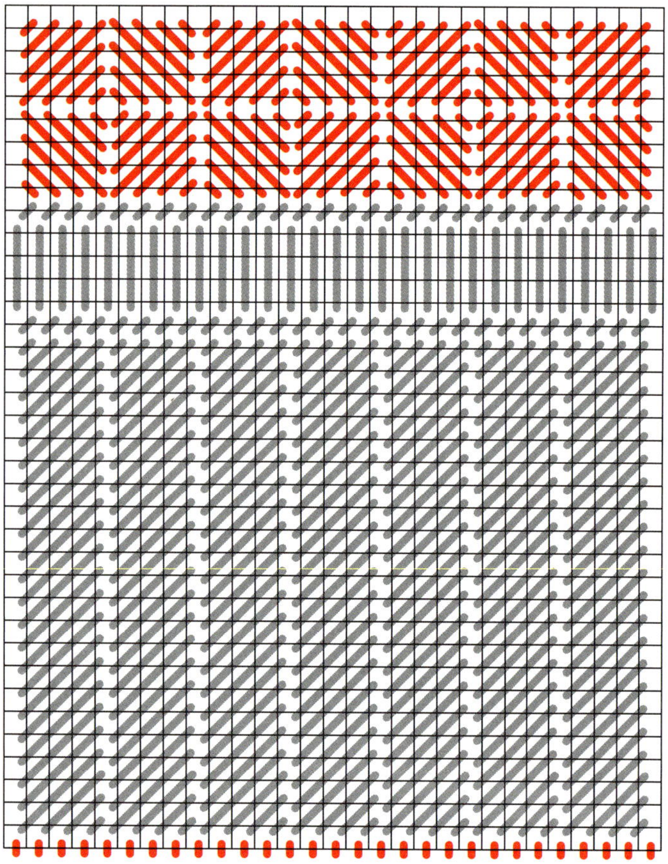

Top (30 x 30 threads)

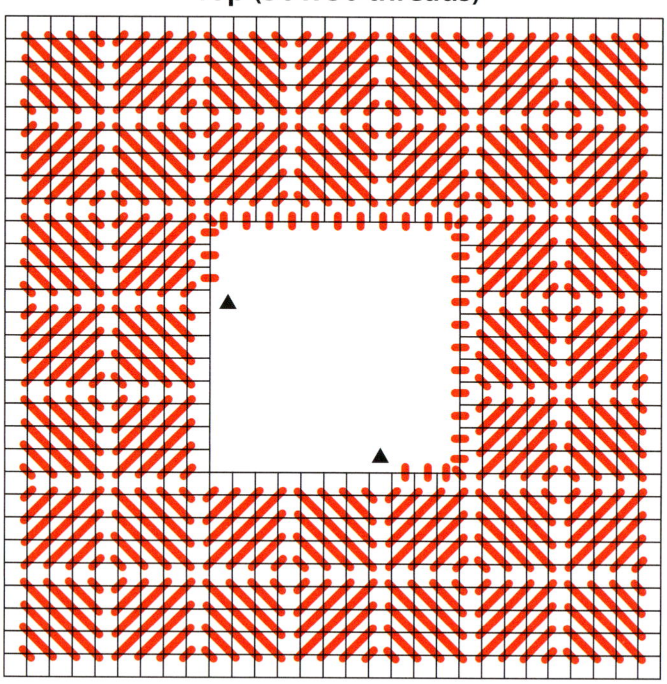

Color Key

- white
- yellow
- red
- dk red
- blue
- black Fr. Knot

Bird Feet (8 x 8 threads)

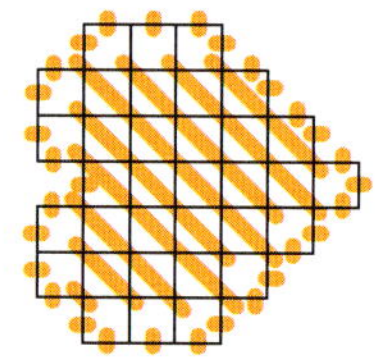

Beak (4 x 4 threads)

Bird Front (17 x 17 threads)

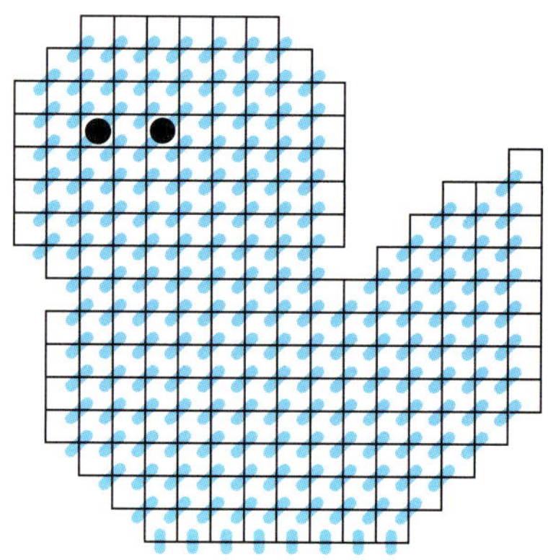

Bird Back (17 x 17 threads)

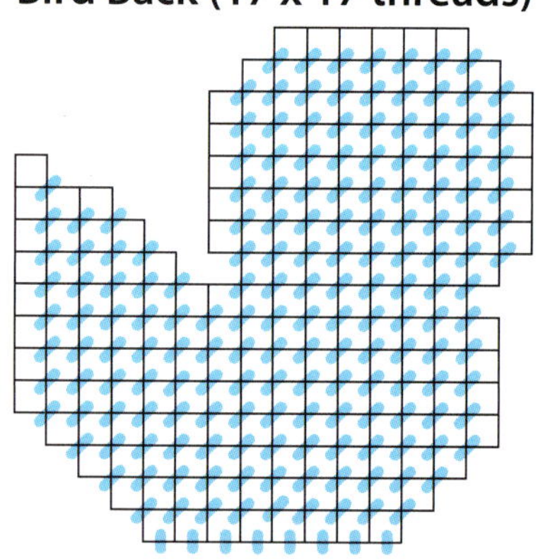

Back Wing (11 x 6 threads)

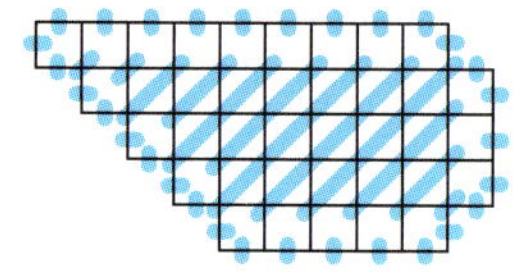

Front Wing (11 x 6 threads)

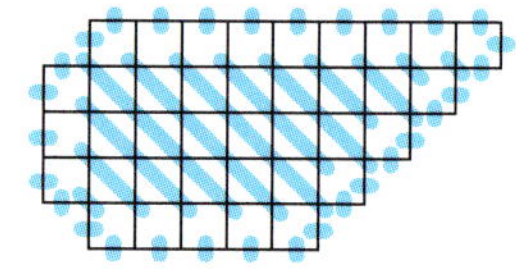

Bird Hat Front (13 x 8 threads)

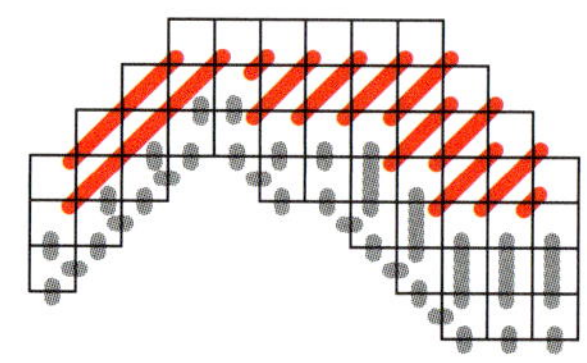

Bird Hat Back (13 x 8 threads)

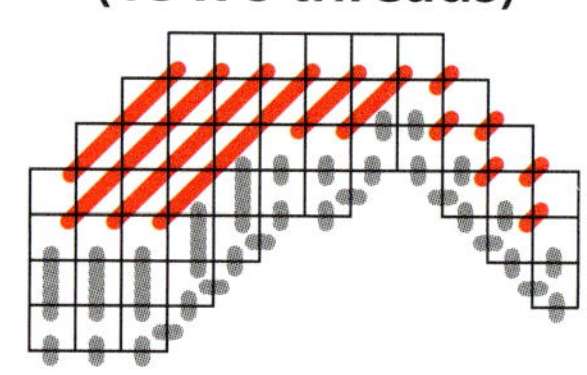

Eyebrows (5 x 4 threads each)

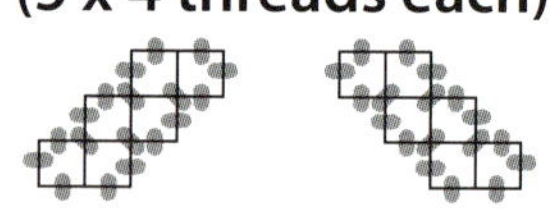

Hat Front (30 x 15 threads)

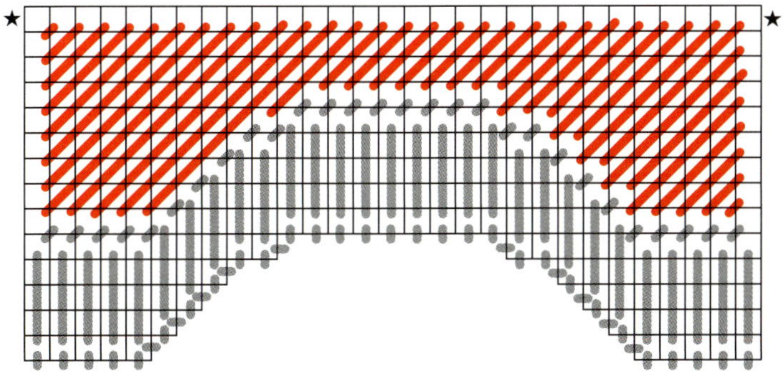

Hat Top (33 x 41 threads)

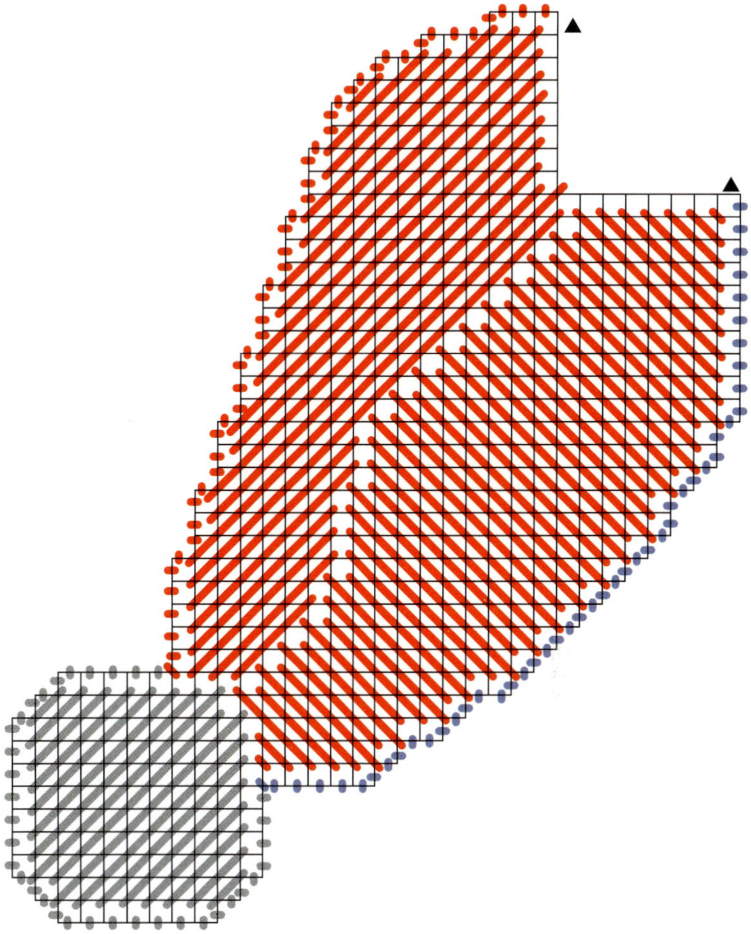

Star (15 x 15 threads) (stitch 2)

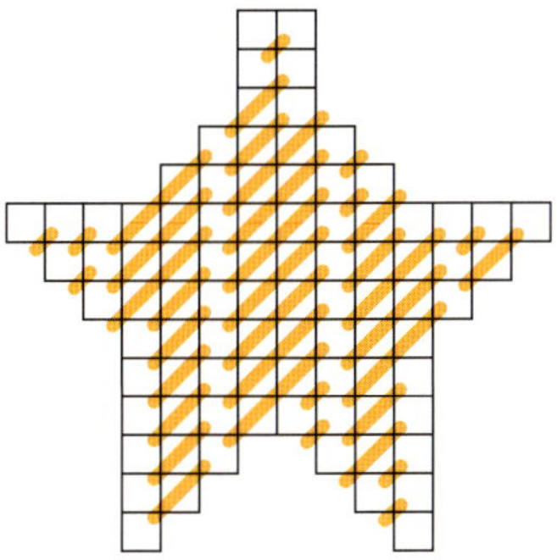

Mustache (22 x 8 threads)

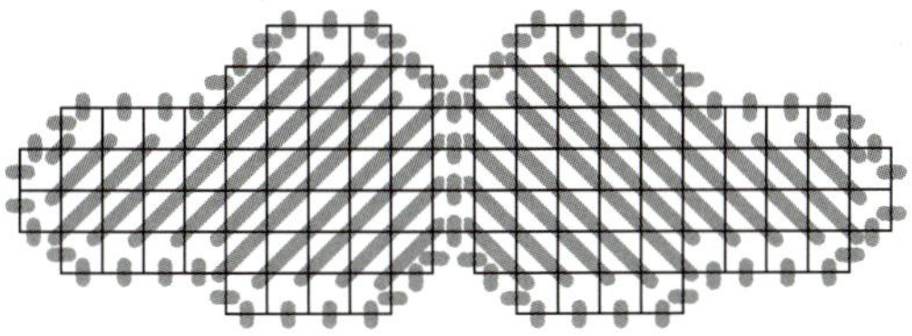

Beard (42 x 23 threads)

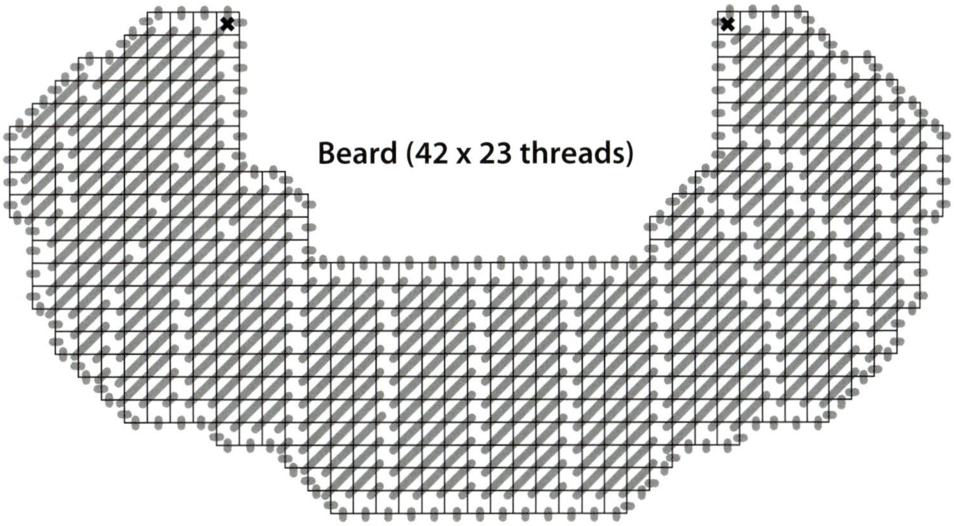

Reindeer Tissue Box Cover

Design by MizFitz.

Size

$6^{1}/_{4}$"w x $11^{1}/_{2}$"h x $4^{3}/_{4}$"d
(fits a $4^{1}/_{4}$"w x $5^{1}/_{4}$"h x $4^{1}/_{4}$"d boutique tissue box)

Supplies

- Two $10^{1}/_{2}$" x $13^{1}/_{2}$" sheets of 7 mesh plastic canvas
- Worsted weight yarn
- #16 tapestry needle

Stitches Used

Alternating Scotch Stitch, Backstitch, French Knot, Gobelin Stitch, Overcast Stitch and Tent Stitch

Instructions

Follow charts to cut and stitch Reindeer Tissue Box Cover Pieces. Using matching color Overcast Stitches, join Sides along long edges. Join Top to Sides. Referring to photo for yarn colors, cover unworked edges of Face. Tack Face to one Side.

For Bird, tack Beak and Wings to Bird pieces. Using red Overcast Stitches, join Bird pieces along unworked edges. Tack Bird to Feet. Tack Feet to Top.

Referring to photo, tack Holly pieces and Tail to tissue box cover.

Beak
(4 x 4 threads)

Feet
(10 x 10 threads)

Side (30 x 37 threads) (stitch 4)

Wing Front
(11 x 6 threads)

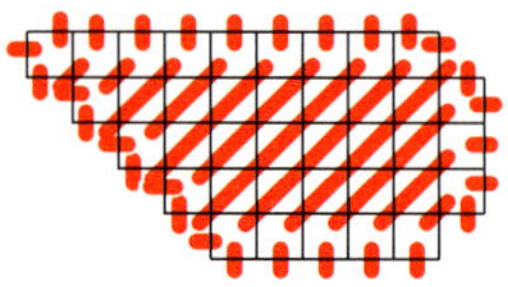

Wing Back
(11 x 6 threads)

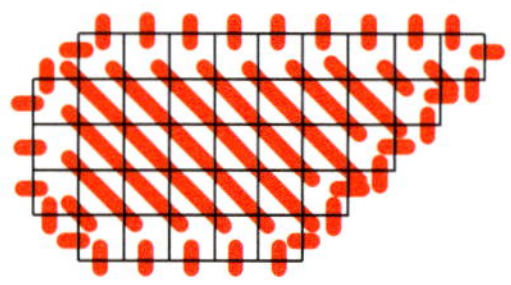

Bird Front
(17 x 17 threads)

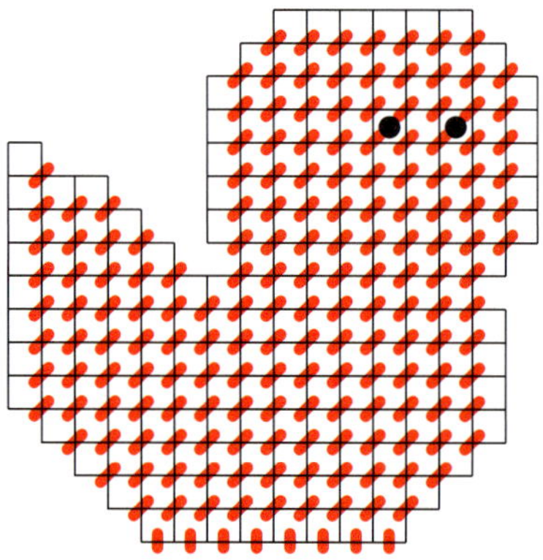

Top (30 x 30 threads)

Bird Back
(17 x 17 threads)

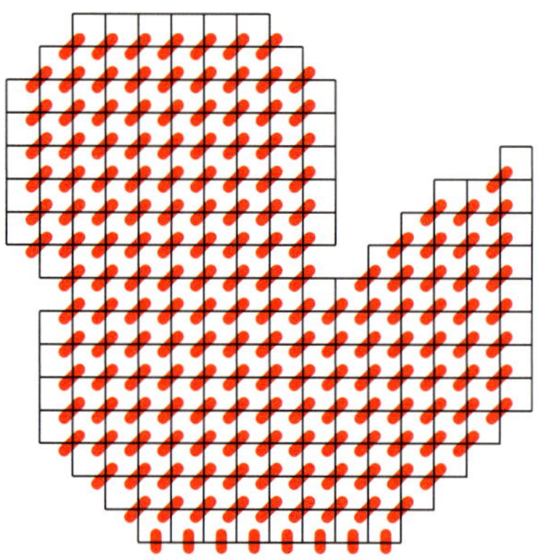

Holly (13 x 13 threads) (stitch 2)

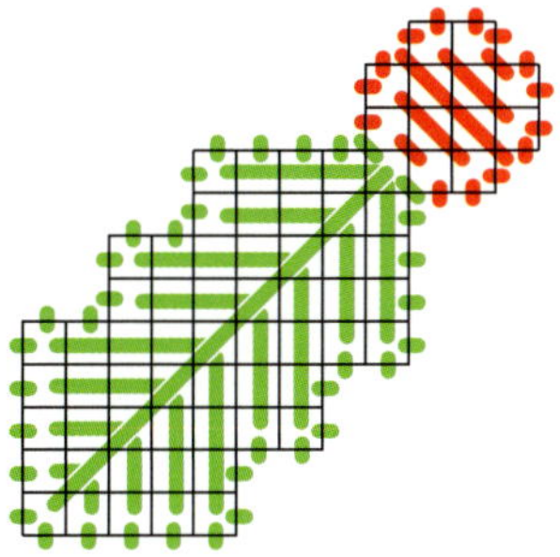

Tail (11 x 14 threads)

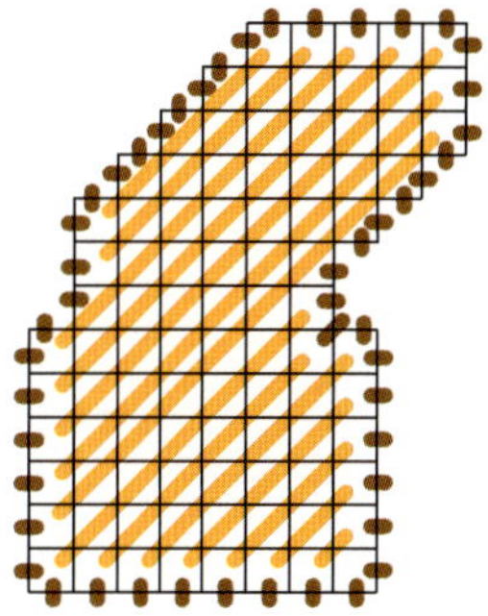

Face (42 x 56 threads)

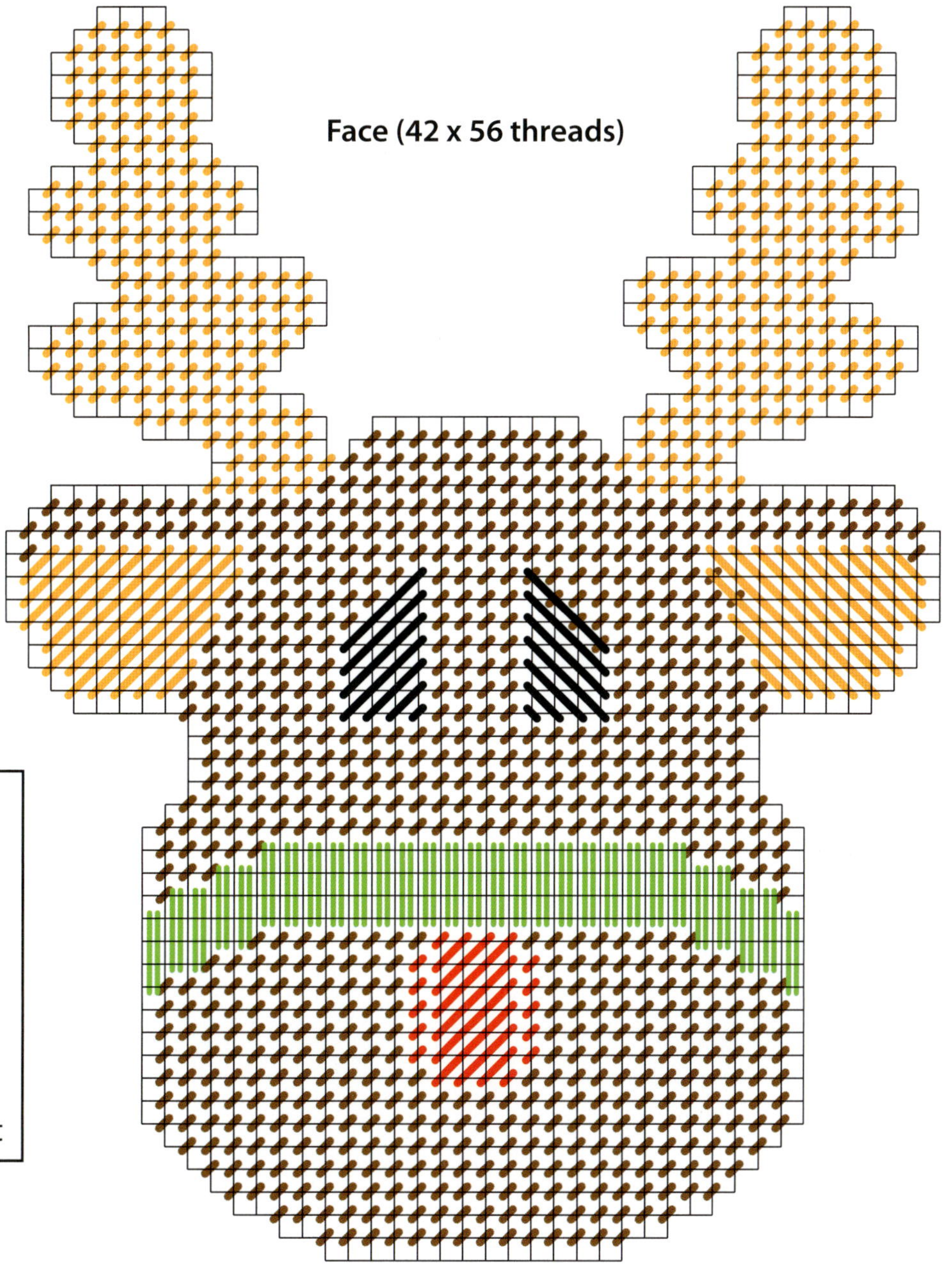

Color Key

- yellow
- red
- green
- lt tan
- tan
- black
- black Fr. Knot

Sleigh Table Decoration

Design by MizFitz.

Size

20"w x 11"h x 7"d

Supplies

- Three 10 1/2" x 13 1/2" sheets of 7 mesh plastic canvas
- Two 3" dia. plastic canvas circle shapes
- Worsted weight yarn
- #16 tapestry needle
- Eight wooden skewers
- 1 yd of 1/8"wide green ribbon for reindeer
- Two 8" lengths of assorted ribbon for gifts
- 1 yd of metallic gold cord
- Four 8mm gold beads
- Four 3/8" gold jingle bells
- Two 8mm moving eyes
- 1/4" pink pom-pom
- Polyester fiberfill
- Clear-drying craft glue

Stitches Used

Alternating Scotch Stitch, Backstitch, French Knot, Gobelin Stitch, Overcast Stitch, and Tent Stitch

Instructions

Follow charts to cut and stitch Sleigh Table Decoration pieces. Use matching color Overcast Stitches for all joining and to cover unworked edges, unless otherwise noted.

For Sleigh, match ☆'s and ♣'s and join Bottom to Sides. Join short edges of one Runner Support along top edge of runner at ✖'s. Join remaining Runner Support along bottom edge of runner at ★'s.

For Santa, join Front to Sides. Tack Arms to Sides. Tack Head to Front along edge of beard. Join Back to Sides. Glue eyes, pom-pom, Mustache, and Eyebrows to Face.

For Santa's Bag, cut circles in half. Circles are not stitched. Join one half circle to Bag at ▲'s. Tack remaining half circle to center of Bag at ✱'s. Tack Bag to Santa. Stuff Santa with fiberfill. Referring to photo, tack Santa to bottom of sleigh.

Referring to photo for yarn colors, cover unworked edges of each reindeer Face.

To assemble each reindeer, match ✖'s and join Front and Back to Body. Tack Face to Front. Tack Tail to Back. Join Bottom to Body. Thread an 8" length of ribbon through bell shank. Tie ribbon in a bow; trim ends. Glue ribbon to Reindeer.

For Bird, join Bird pieces along unworked edges. Tack Feet to Bird. Glue Wings and Beak to Bird.

Glue Heart to one reindeer. Glue Bird to one reindeer.

Use white Overcast Stitches to join Checked Gift pieces along unworked edges, forming a cube. Cover unworked edges of Green Gift. Join Blue Gift Side along short edges. Join Blue Gift Top and Bottom to Blue Gift Side along unworked edges. For each Bear, tack Bear Paws and Feet to Bear. Tack Star to Tree.

For bows on Gifts and Bears, tie an 8" length of yarn or ribbon in a bow; trim ends. Glue bows to Gifts and Bears.

Referring to photo, thread cord through Santa's mittens and through each reindeer. Tuck ends behind reindeer heads; glue in place. Glue beads to Sleigh.

Glue skewer to the wrong side of Tree, Gifts, Bears, and Candy Canes. Referring to photo, trim skewers to different lengths. Insert skewers into unstitched half circles in Santa's Bag. Adjust lengths of skewers as desired.

Color Key
- green
- black

Sleigh Side #1
(61 x 38 threads)

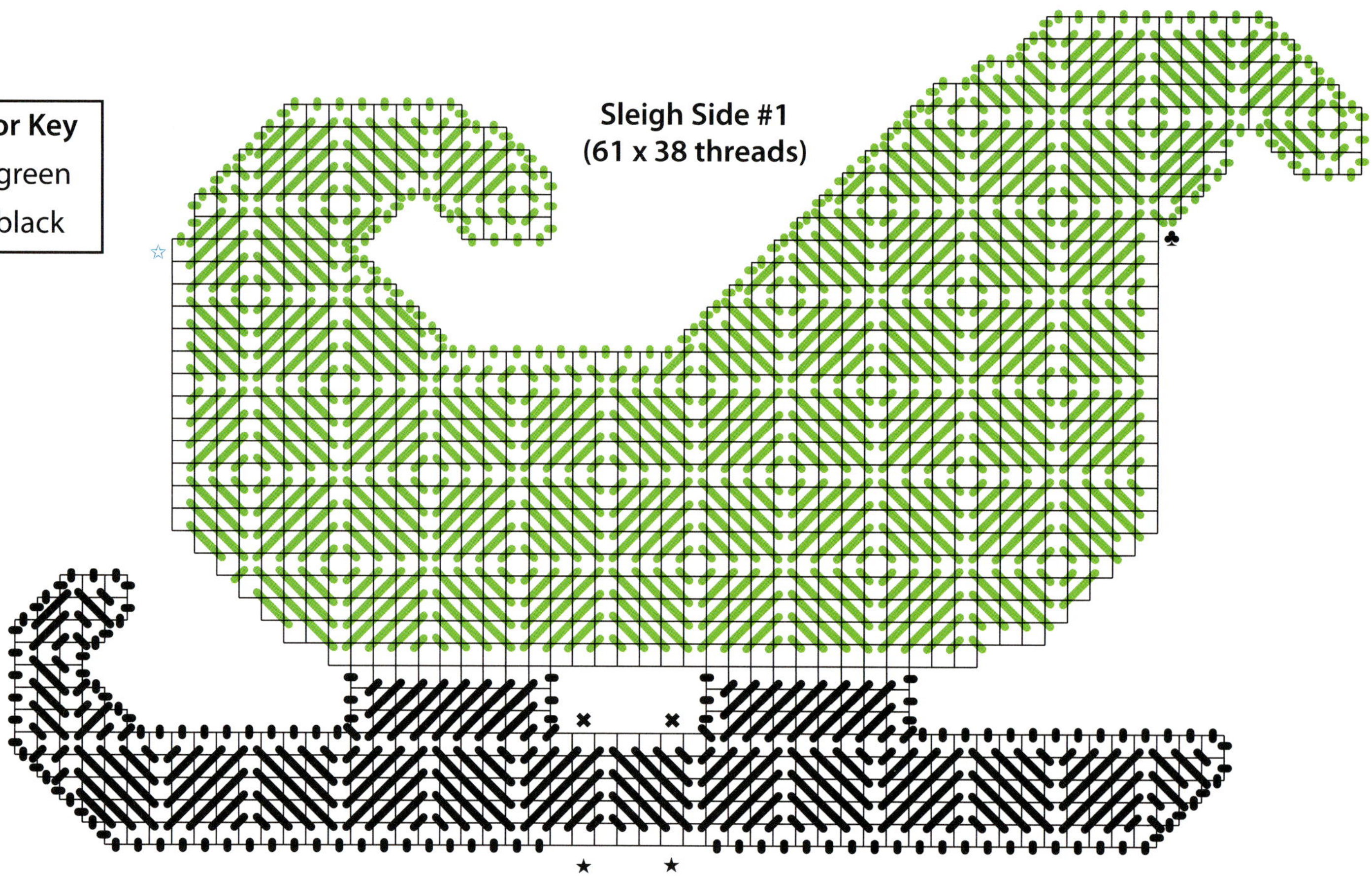

Santa Back (20 x 30 threads)

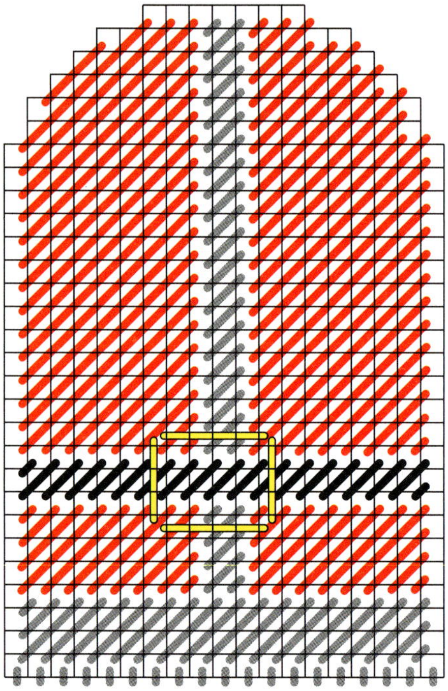

Santa Arm (18 x 14 threads)

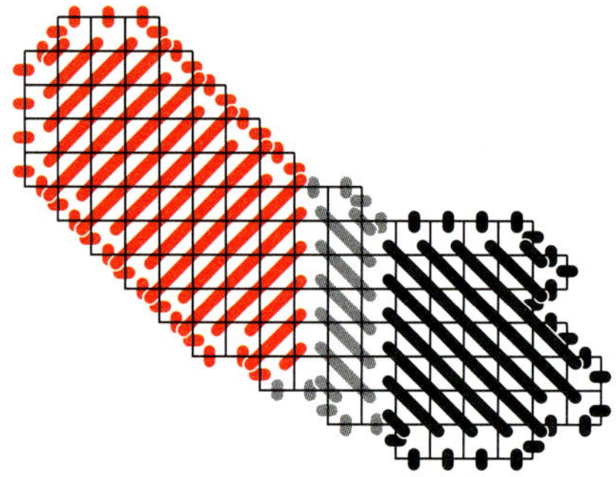

Santa Side (13 x 70 threads)

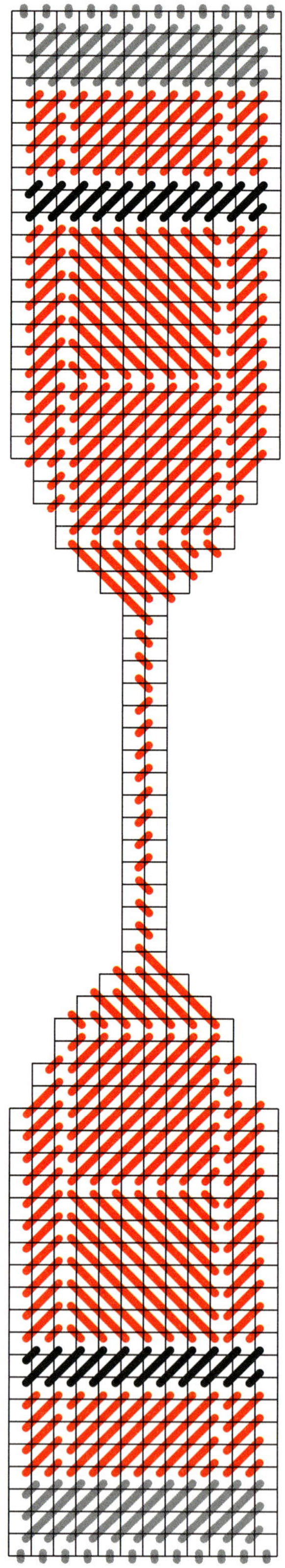

Santa Arm (18 x 14 threads)

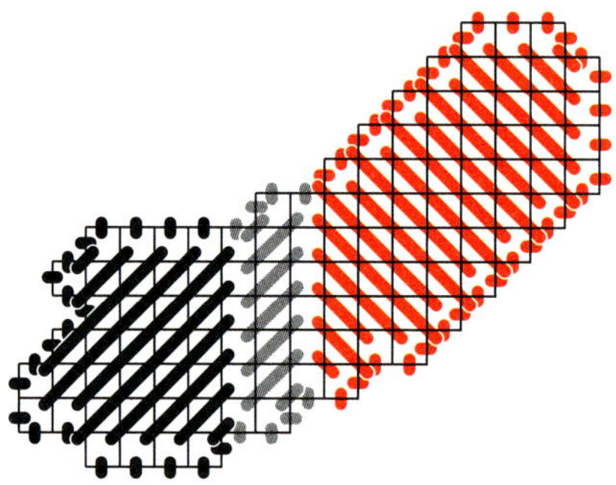

Santa Front (20 x 30 threads)

Color Key

white	red
yellow	green
peach	dk red
rose	black

Sleigh Side #2
(61 x 38 threads)

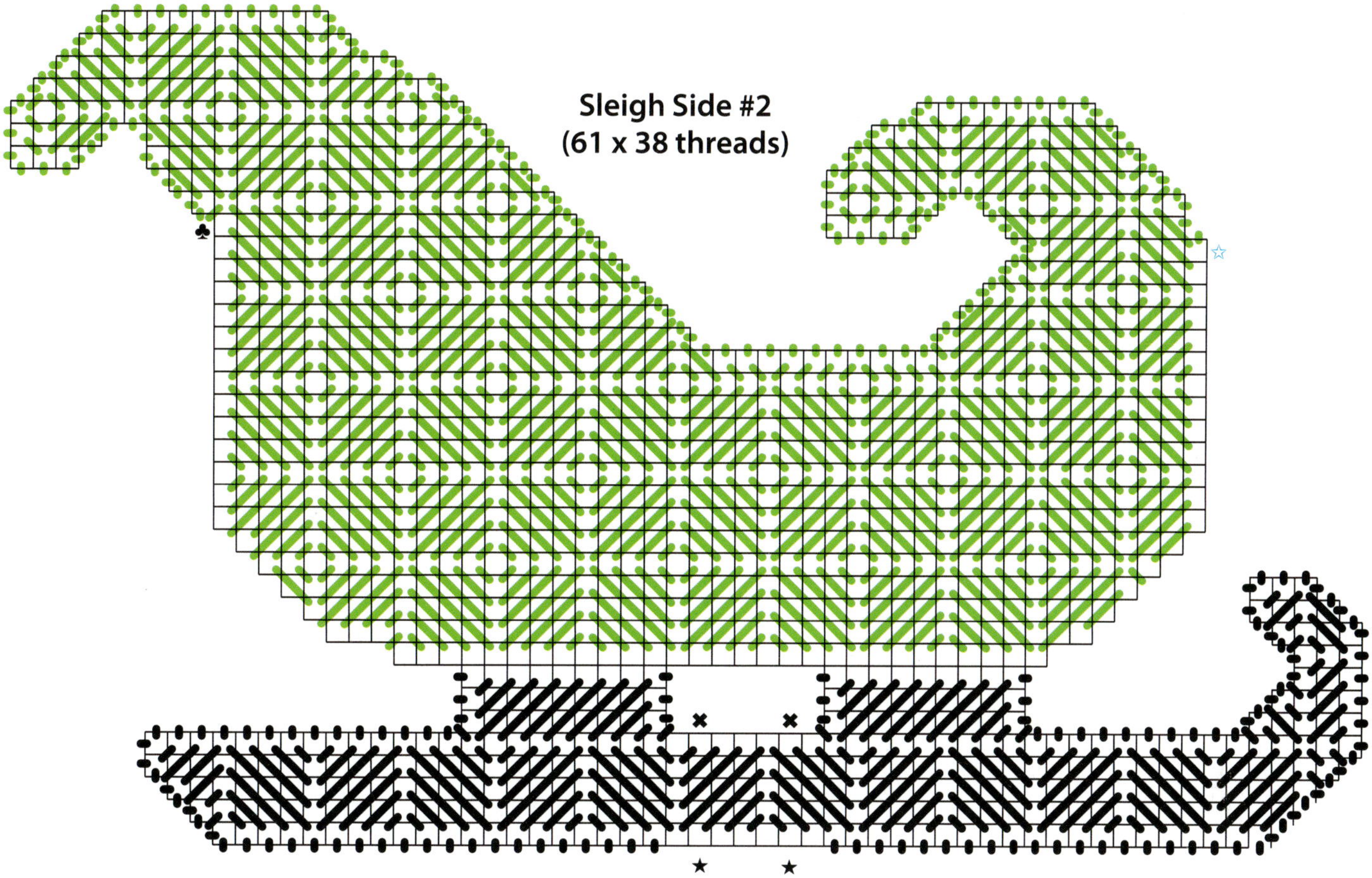

Runner Support (22 x 6 threads) (stitch 2)

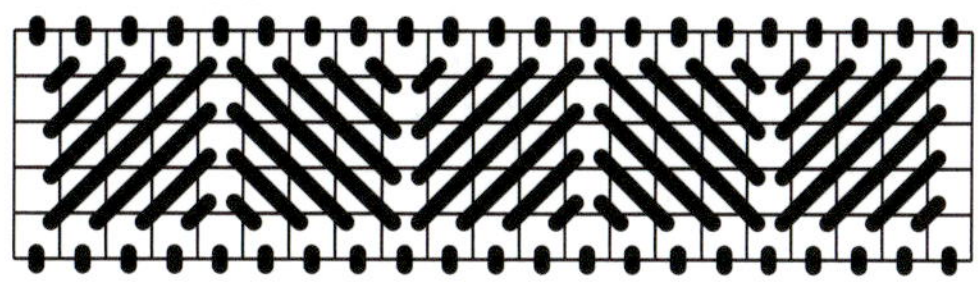

Eyebrows (4 x 3 threads each)

Mustache (10 x 4 threads)

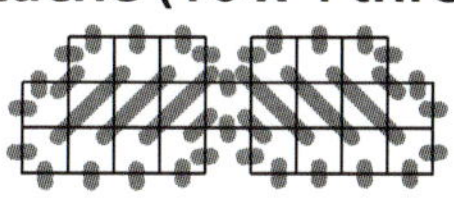

Santa Head (29 x 24 threads)

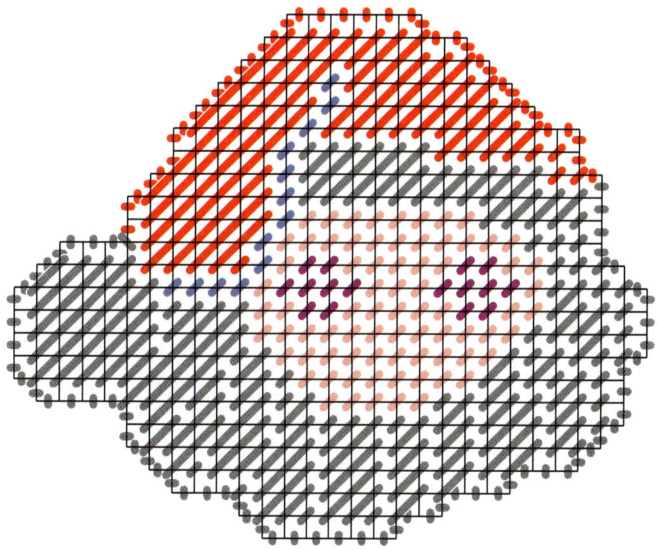

Bag (44 x 17 threads)

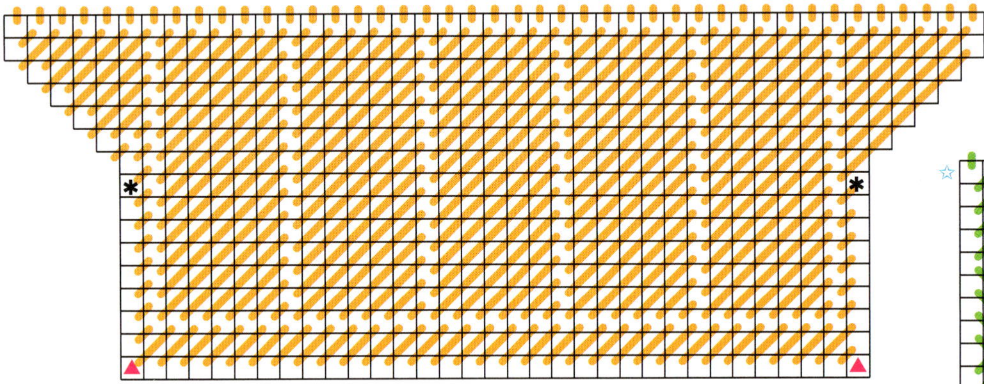

Blue Gift Top/Bottom (10 x 10 threads) (stitch 2)

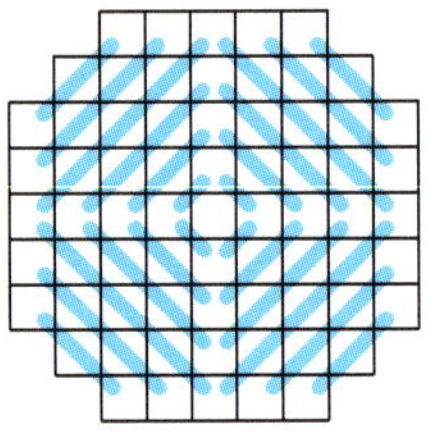

Blue Gift Side (31 x 5 threads)

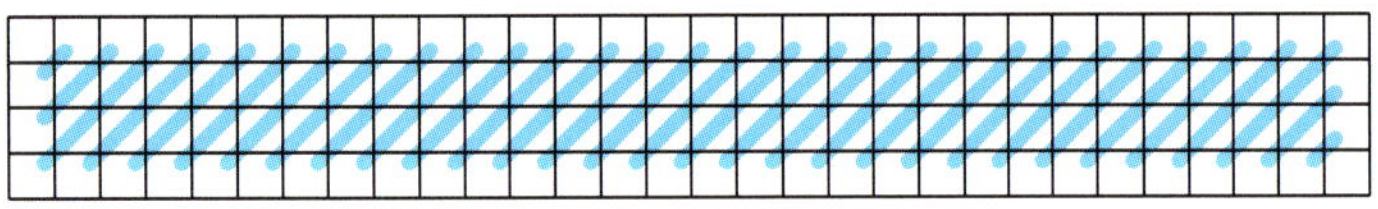

Color Key

- white
- yellow
- rose
- red
- green
- lt tan
- tan
- black
- blue Fr. Knot
- black Fr. Knot

Sleigh Bottom (22 x 76 threads)

Checked Gift (10 x 10 threads) (stitch 6)

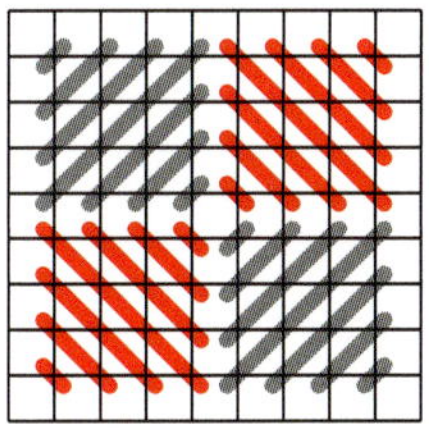

Star (10 x 10 threads)

Green Gift (8 x 20 threads) (cut 4; stack and stitch through all 4 layers)

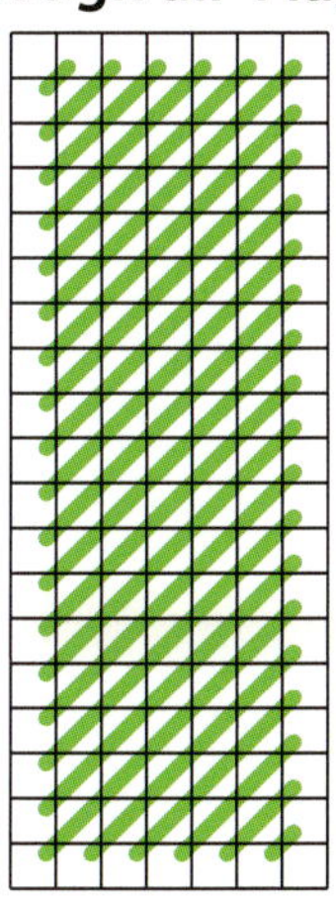

Bear Paw A (4 x 4 threads) (stitch 2)

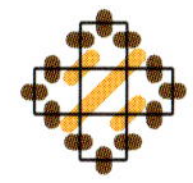

Bear Foot A (5 x 6 threads) (stitch 2)

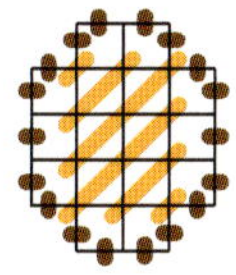

Bear A (11 x 16 threads

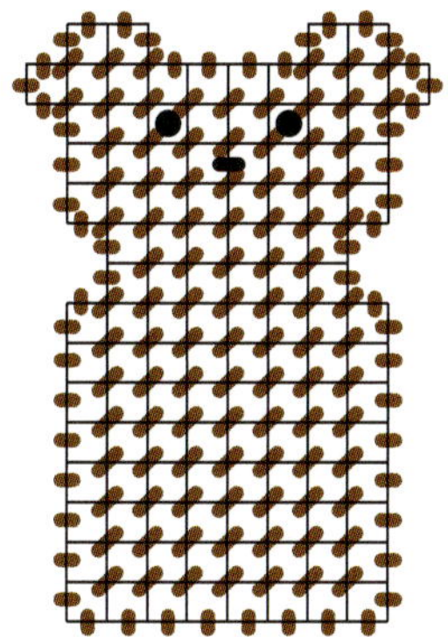

Bear B Paw (4 x 4 threads) (stitch 2)

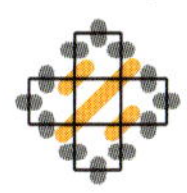

Bear B Foot (5 x 6 threads) (stitch 2)

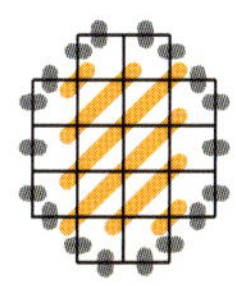

Bear B (11 x 16 threads

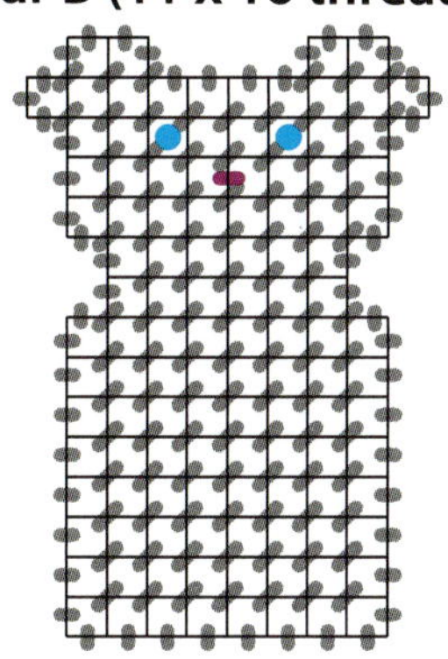

Candy Cane (11 x 20 threads)

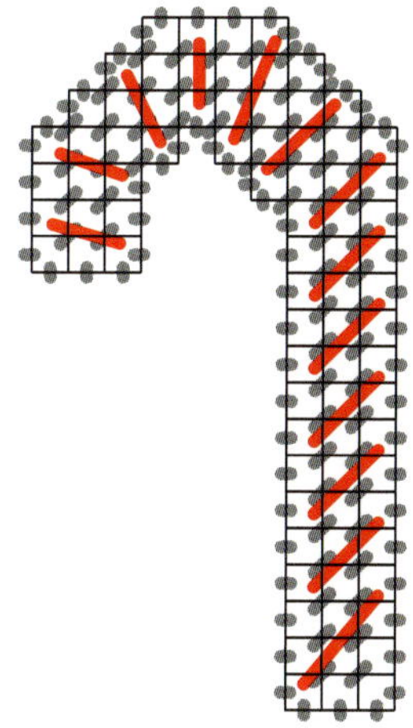

Candy Cane (11 x 20 threads)

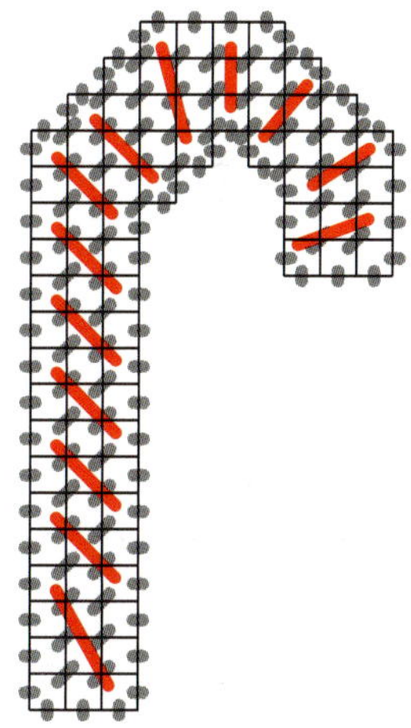

Tree (18 x 29 threads)

Reindeer Face
(26 x 35 threads) (stitch 4)

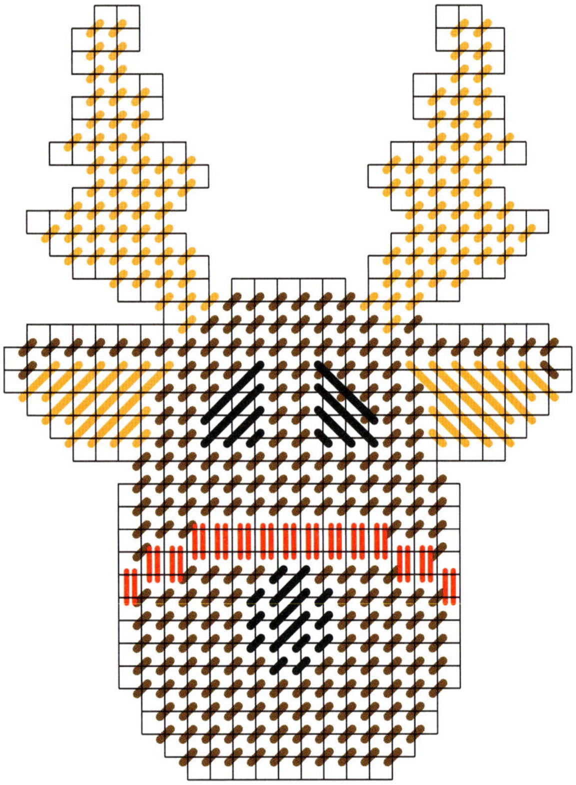

Reindeer Body
(18 x 58 threads) (stitch 4)

Color Key

- yellow
- red
- lt tan
- tan
- black
- black Fr. Knot

Reindeer Front/Back
(18 x 23 threads) (stitch 8)

Reindeer Bottom
(18 x 18 threads) (stitch 4)

Bird Front
(9 x 9 threads)

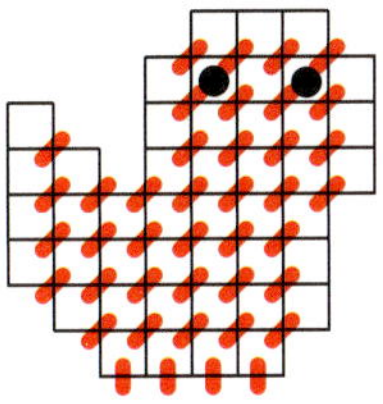

Bird Back
(9 x 9 threads)

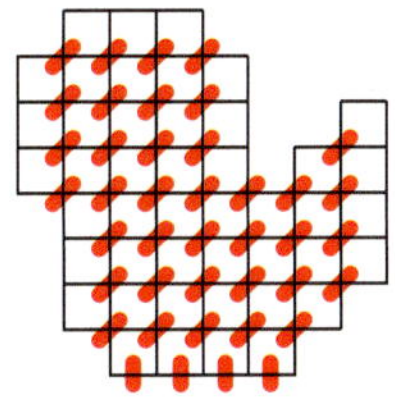

Heart 8 x 8 threads)

Bird Beak
(3 x 3 threads)

Bird Feet
(5 x 5 threads)

Reindeer Tail
(7 x 8 threads) (stitch 4)

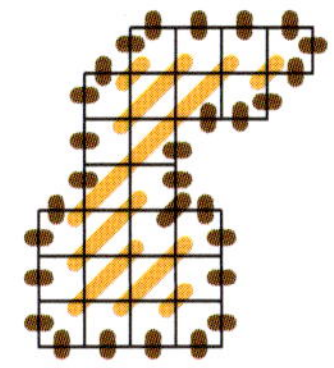

Front Wing
(6 x 4 threads)

Back Wing
(6 x 4 threads)

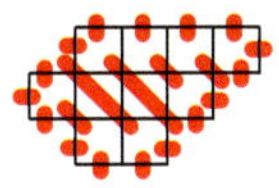

Reindeer & Santa Ornaments

Designs by MizFitz.

Size
approximately 4"w x 4"h each

Supplies
$10\frac{1}{2}$" x $13\frac{1}{2}$" sheets of 7 mesh plastic canvas
Worsted weight yarn
#16 tapestry needle
Clear nylon thread
For Santa only: Two 8mm wiggle eyes, $\frac{1}{4}$" pink pom-pom and craft glue

Stitches Used
Alternating Scotch Stitch, Backstitch, Gobelin Stitch, Overcast Stitch, and Tent Stitch.

Instructions
Reindeer
Follow charts to cut and stitch Reindeer Ornament pieces.

Using matching color Overcast Stitches and matching ✖'s, join long edges of Side to Front and Back. Referring to photo for yarn colors, cover unworked edges of Face. Tack Face to Front. Tack Tail to Back.

For hanger, thread a 12" length of nylon thread through ornament; knot and trim ends.

Using black Overcast Stitches, join Bottom to Front, Back, and Side.

Santa
Follow charts to cut and stitch Santa Ornament pieces.

Using matching color Overcast Stitches, join Hat Back to Hat Front along unworked edges of Front. Tack Hat to Santa's head. Tack Eyebrows and Mustache to Santa. Glue eyes and pom-pom nose to Santa.

For hanger, thread a 12" length of nylon thread through ornament; knot and trim ends.

Front/Back
(14 x 18 threads)
(stitch 2)

Face (18 x 24 threads)

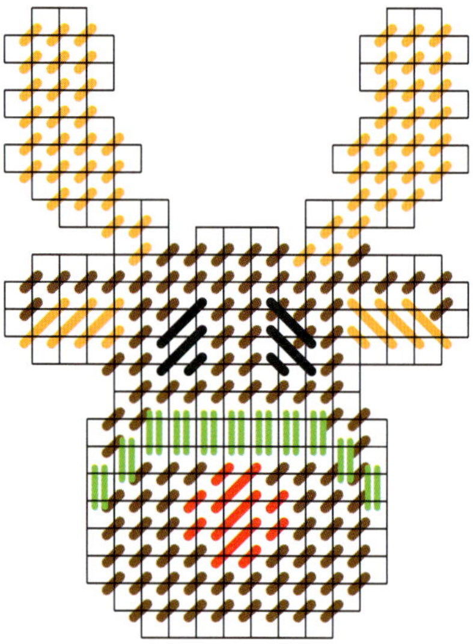

Tail (6 x 7 threads)

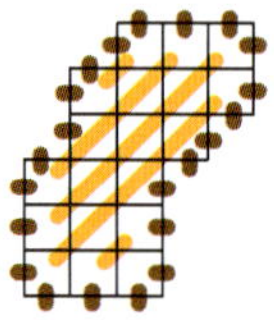

Color Key
- red
- green
- lt tan
- tan
- black

Side (14 x 44 threads)

Bottom (14 x 14 threads)

Santa (26 x 24 threads)

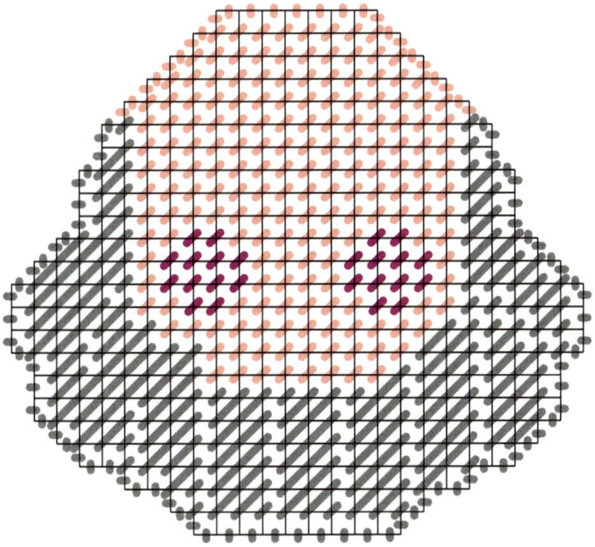

Mustache (11 x 5 threads)

Color Key

- white
- peach
- rose
- red
- dk red

Eyebrows (4 x 3 threads each)

Hat Front/Back
(27 x 17 threads) (cut 2, stitch 1)

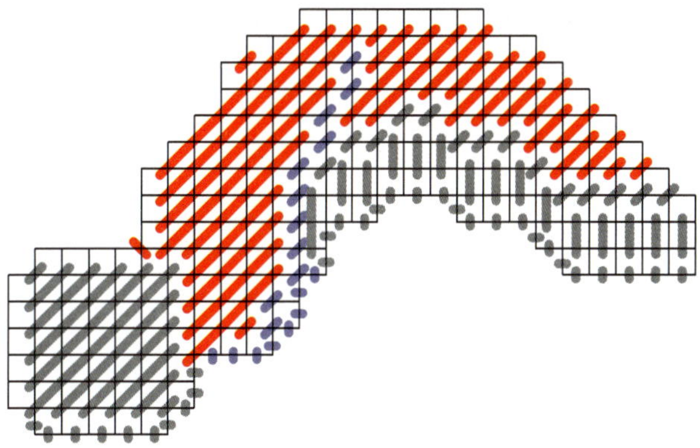

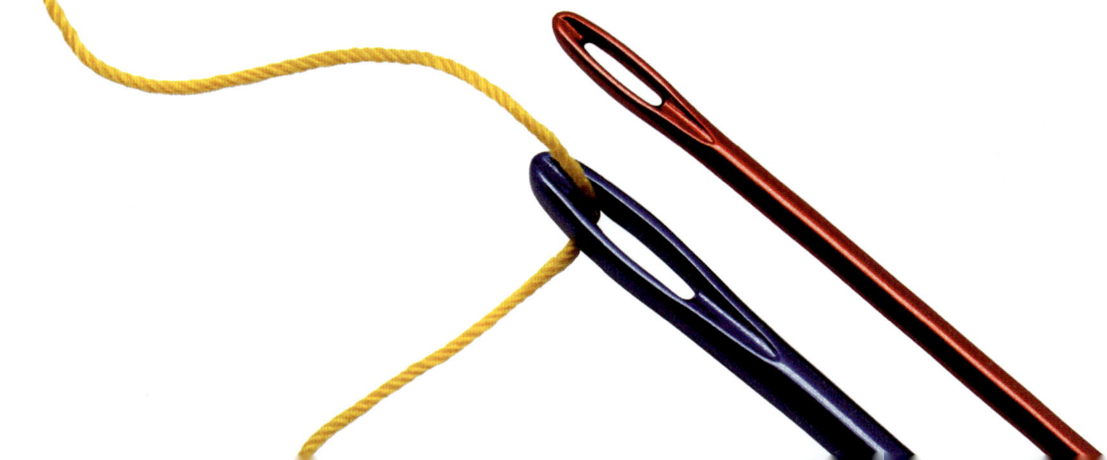

North Pole Lineup

Design by MizFitz.

Size

19"w x 15"h

Supplies

- Six 10½" x 13½" sheets of 7 mesh plastic canvas
- Worsted weight yarn
- #16 tapestry needle
- Four 3" x 10" white foam board rectangles
- Six 12mm wiggle eyes
- One ½" jingle bell
- Three ¼" jingle bells
- Six red buttons
- 17" length metallic gold ribbon
- Four 6mm gold beads
- Powder blush
- Craft glue

Stitches Used

Alternating Scotch Stitch, Backstitch, French Knot, Gobelin Stitch, Overcast Stitch, and Tent Stitch

Color Key

red

Hinge (14 x 7 threads) (stitch 6)

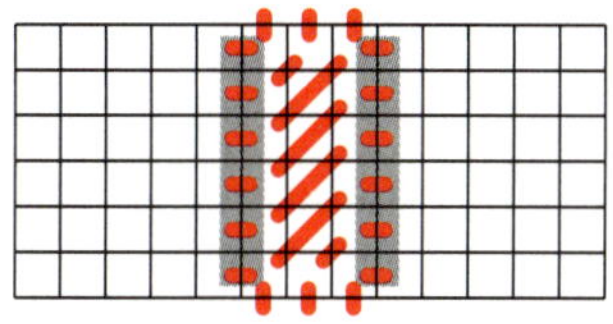

Joining the Characters

After all characters are stitched, work stitches in pink shaded areas to cover unworked edges of Fronts only. Insert Hinges in openings on piece sides. Work stitches in grey shaded areas to join Hinges to unworked edges of Backs only.

Reindeer

Follow charts to cut and stitch pieces, leaving shaded areas unworked. Tack Large Heart, Bow, and Head to Reindeer Front. Cut a 12" length of dk green yarn. Thread yarn through 1/2" jingle bell. Insert both ends of yarn through Reindeer Head from front to back. Insert both ends of yarn back through Reindeer Head from back to front. Tie bow; trim ends. Placing foam board rectangle between Reindeer Front and Back, use matching color Overcast Stitches to join unshaded edges of Reindeer Front and Back.

Santa

Follow charts to cut and stitch pieces, leaving shaded areas unworked. Tack Nose and top edge of Mustache to Santa Front. Glue eyes to Santa Front. Glue buttons to Wreath. Tie a 9" length of red yarn in a bow; glue to Wreath. Insert Arms through Wreath; tack Arms and Wreath to Santa Front.

Matching ★'s, tack bottom edge of Hat to Santa Front. Working stitches in yellow shaded area and stitching through three layers of canvas, join Hat to Santa Front and Back. Glue Eyebrows to Hat and Santa Front. Tack Pom-pom to Hat.

Matching ♥'s, work stitches in green shaded areas through three layers of canvas to join Beard to Santa Front and Back. Matching ▲'s, tack top of Shoes to Santa Front. Place foam board rectangle between Santa Front and Back. Working stitches in blue shaded area and stitching through three layers of canvas, join Shoes to Santa Front and Back. Using matching color Overcast Stitches, join unshaded edges of Santa Front and Back. Apply blush to Santa's face.

Mrs. Santa

Follow charts to cut and stitch pieces, leaving shaded areas unworked. Tack Nose and Lace to Mrs. Santa Front. Tack Small Heart to Apron; tack Apron to Mrs. Santa Front. Tack Leaves to Hat Brim; tack Hat Brim to Mrs. Santa Front. Tack Cookies to Cookie Sheet; tack Cookie Sheet to Arms; tack Arms to Apron and Mrs. Santa Front. Glue eyes to Mrs. Santa Front.

Placing foam board rectangle between Mrs. Santa Front and Back, use matching color Overcast Stitches to join unshaded edges of Mrs. Santa Front and Back. Apply blush to Mrs. Santa's face.

Elf

Follow charts to cut and stitch pieces, leaving shaded areas unworked. Tack Nose and Ears to Elf Front. Glue eyes to Elf Front. Tack beads to Elf Front.

Using bright green Overcast Stitches, join Box Sides along short edges. Join Box Top and Bottom to Sides along long edges. Tack Box to wrong side of Arms. Tack Arms to Elf Front. Tie bow with ribbon; glue ribbon to Box, Arms, and Elf Front.

Turn Shoes over. Referring to Elf Shoes Diagram, work stitches in blue shaded areas on wrong side of Shoes. Turn piece to the right side and tack tips of Shoes to the front of the Shoes. Tack 1/4" jingle bells to tips.

Matching ■'s, tack top of Shoes to Elf Front. Place foam board rectangle between Elf Front and Back. Working stitches in yellow shaded area and stitching through three layers of canvas, join Shoes to Elf Front and Back. Referring to photo for yarn colors, use Overcast Stitches to join unshaded edges of Elf Front and Back.

Tack 1/4" jingle bell to tip of hat. Apply blush to Elf's face.

Reindeer Front/Back
(30 x 78 threads) (cut 2) (stitch 1)

Large Heart
(12 x 12 threads)

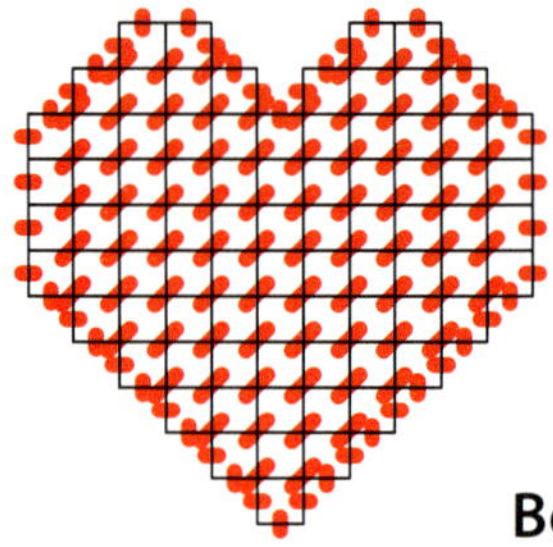

Color Key

- white
- red
- peach
- tan
- brown
- green
- dk green
- black
- red Fr. Knot

Bow (17 x 10 threads)

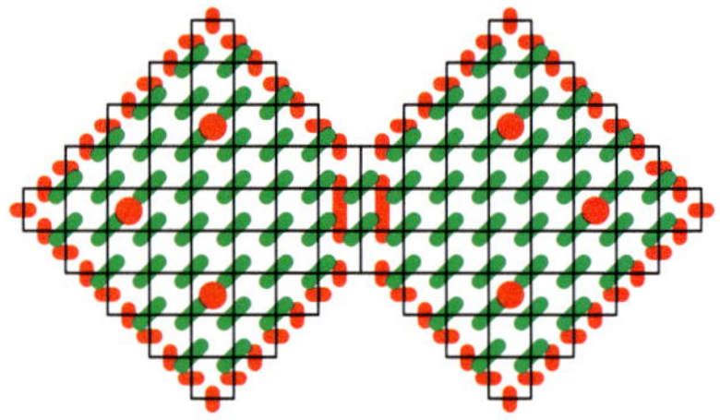

Reindeer Head
(30 x 55 threads)

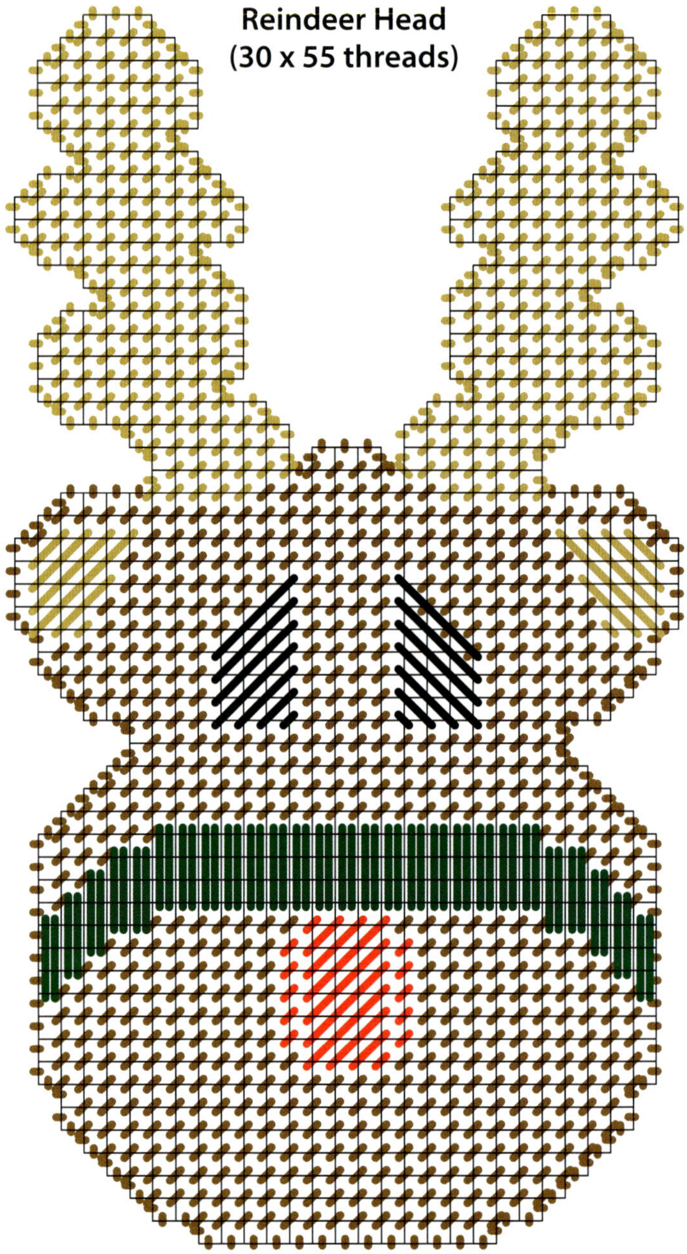

Santa Front/Back
(30 x 89 threads)
(cut 2) (stitch 1)

Santa Eyebrows
(4 x 4 threads each)

Santa Nose (4 x 4 threads) (cut 2)
Stack and stitch through two layers of canvas.

Pom-pom
(8 x 8 threads)

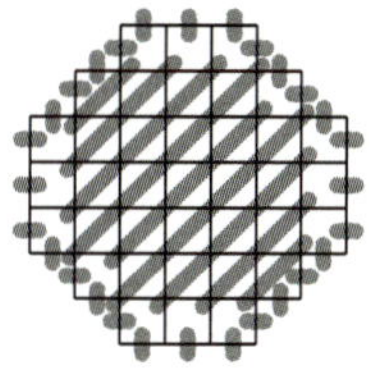

Mustache
(13 x 4 threads)

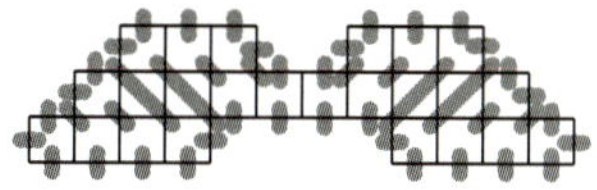

Wreath (24 x 24 threads)

Santa Shoes (30 x 10 threads)

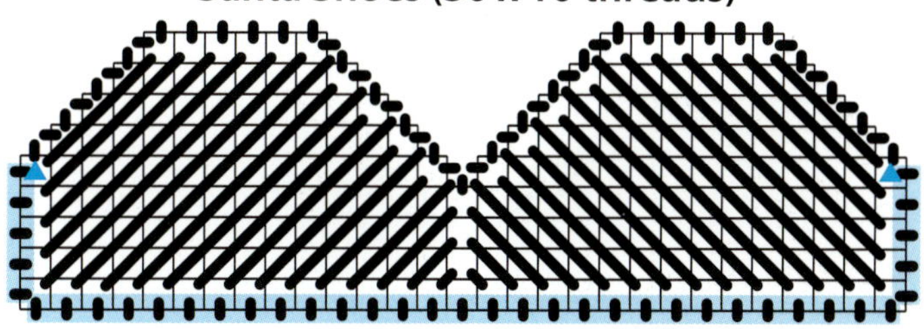

Beard (26 x 13 threads)
After working overcast stitches, tie 4" lengths of white yarn to threads to cover Beard; trim ends.

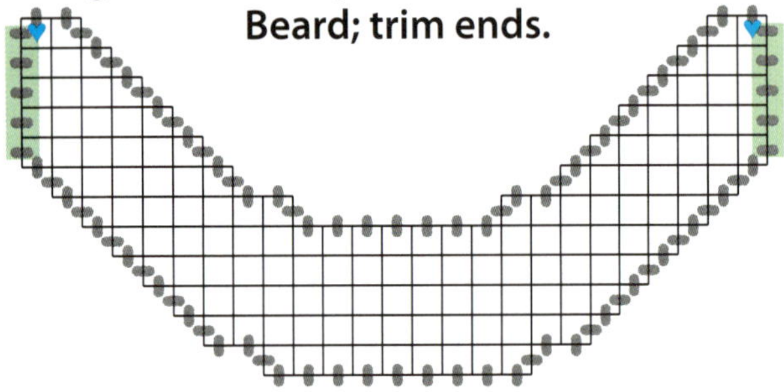

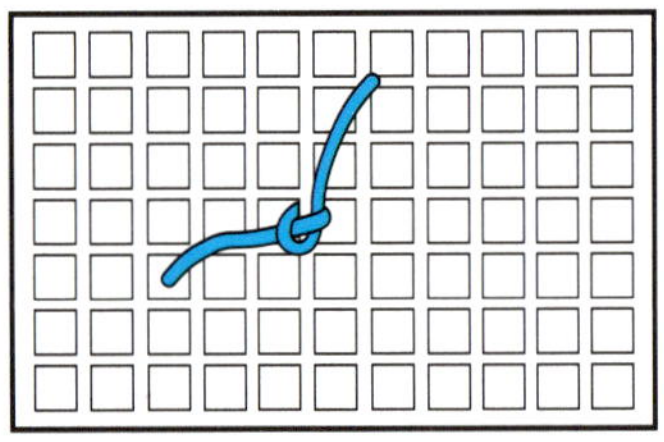

Santa Hat (27 x 19 threads)

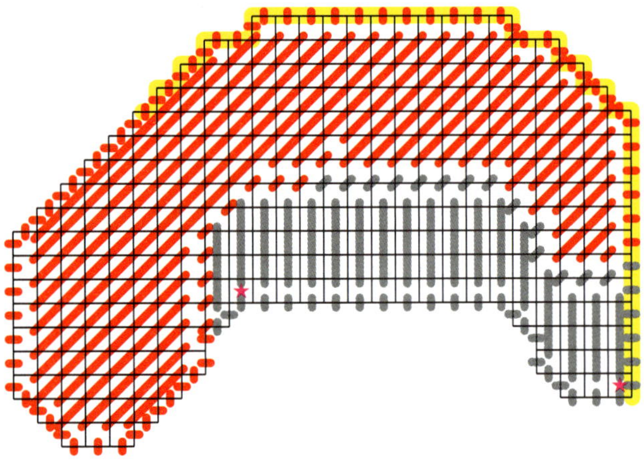

Santa Arms
(30 x 23 threads)

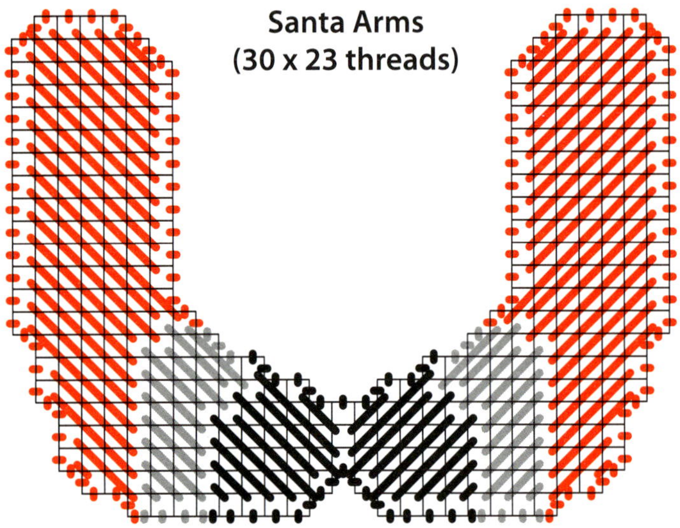

Mrs. Santa Front/Back
(30 x 85 threads)
(cut 2) (stitch 1)

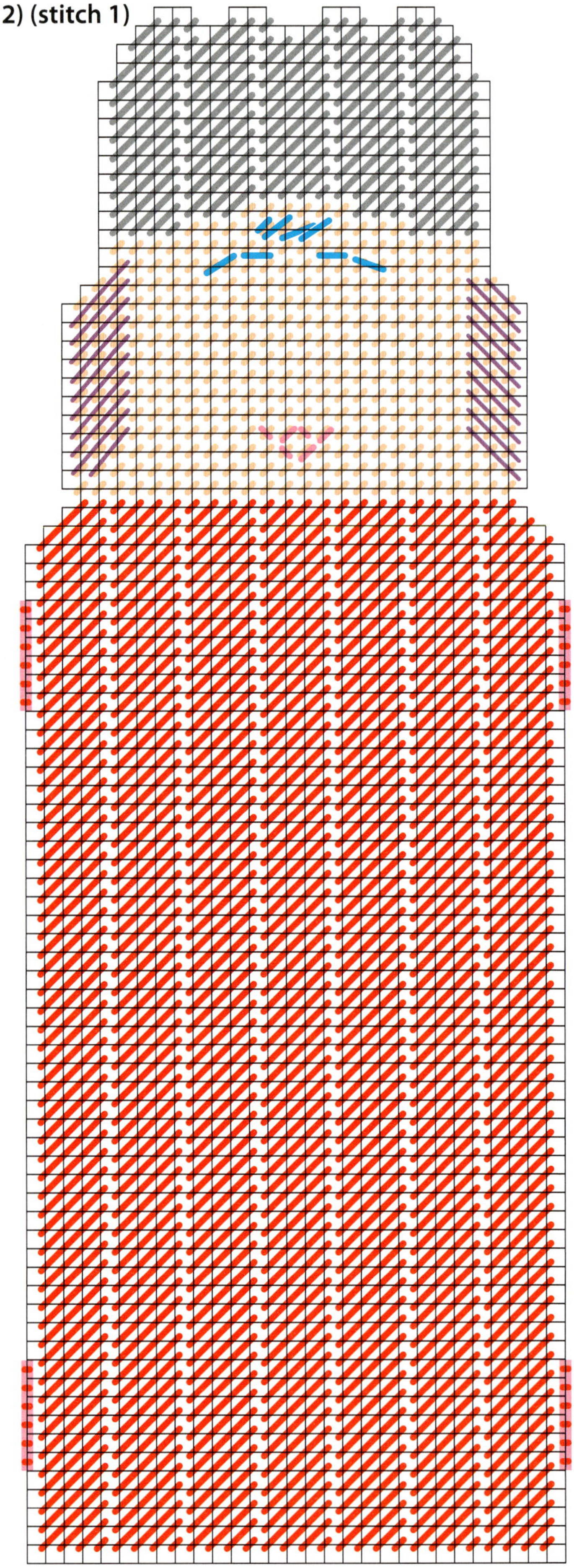

Color Key

- white
- peach
- rose
- red
- green
- dk brown
- lt grey
- lt grey (use 2 strands)
- pink
- red Fr. Knot

Mrs. Santa Hat Brim (28 x 11 threads)

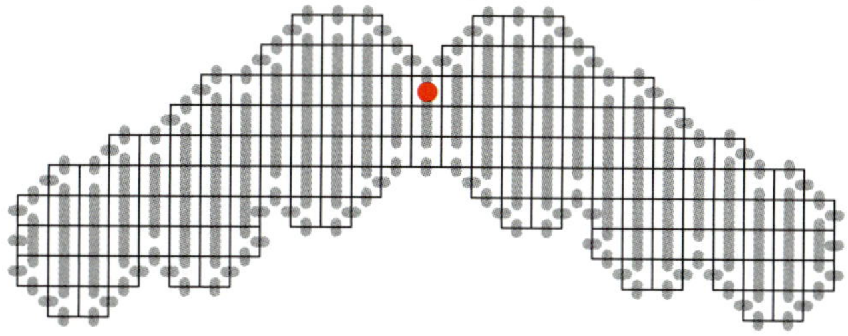

Mrs. Santa Nose (4 x 4 threads) (cut 2)

Stack and stitch through two layers of canvas.

Boy Cookie (7 x 10 threads)

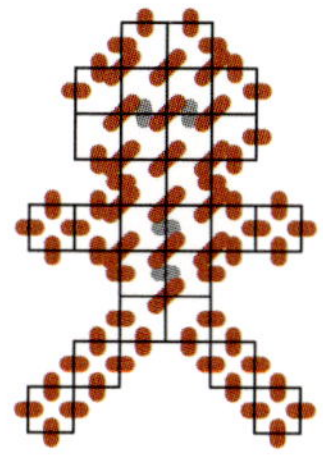

Girl Cookie (7 x 10 threads)

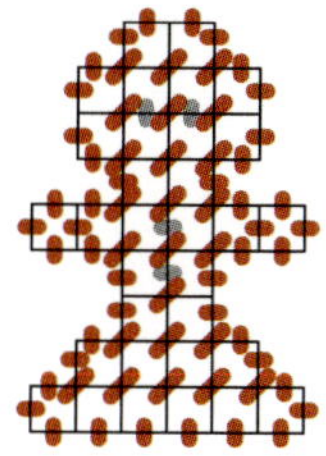

Small Heart (8 x 7 threads)

Mrs. Santa Leaf (6 x 4 threads) (stitch 2)

Cookie Sheet (17 x 12 threads)

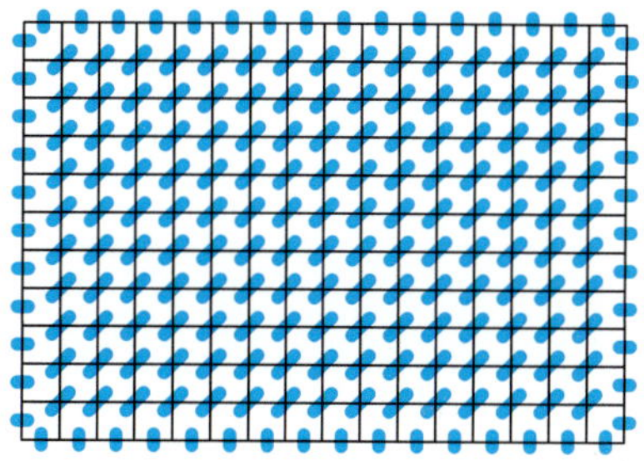

Mrs. Santa Apron (30 x 46 threads)

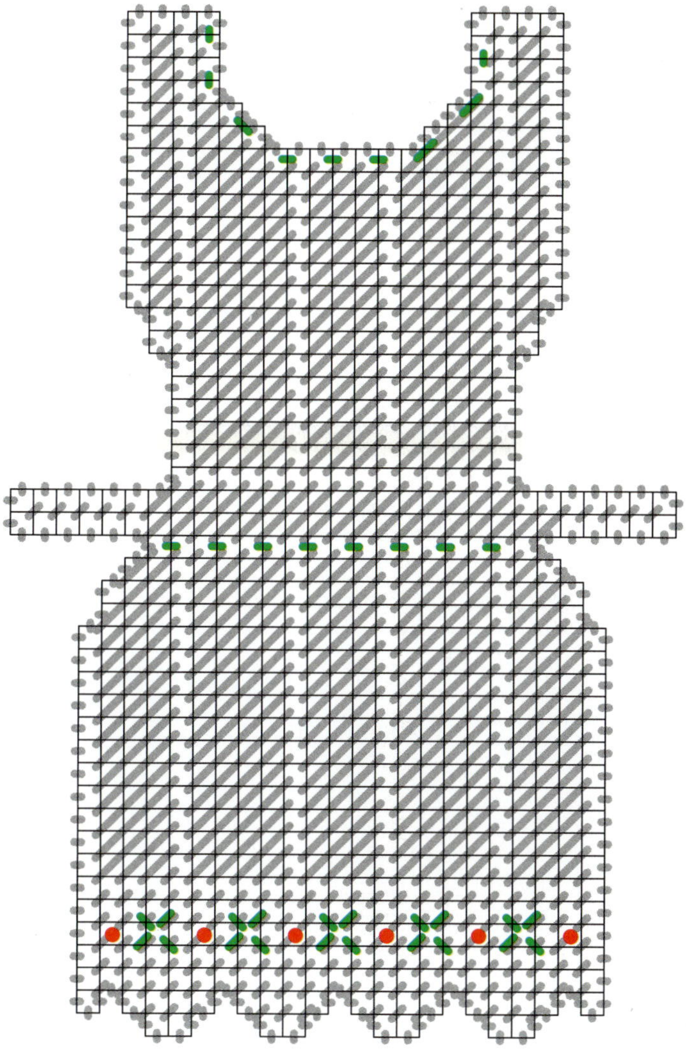

Mrs. Santa Lace (30 x 5 threads)

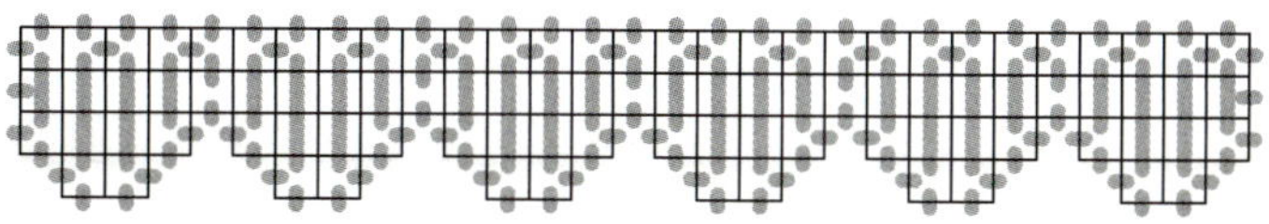

Mrs. Santa Arms (30 x 20 threads)

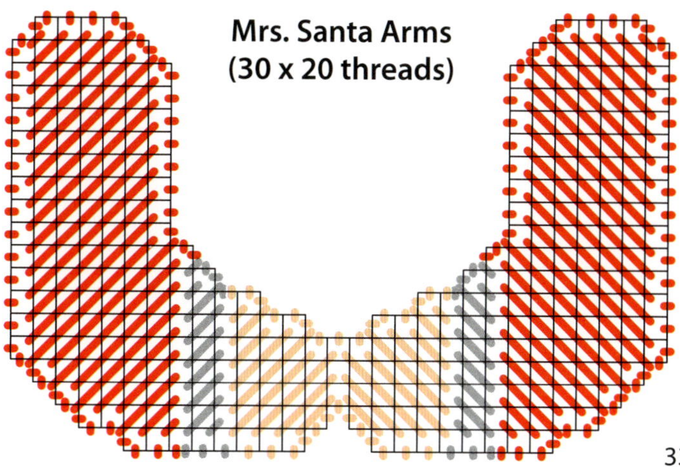

Color Key

white	rose	dk red	dk green	dk brown
peach	red	bright green	brown	black

Box Side
(3 x 9 threads) (stitch 4)

Box Top/Bottom
(9 x 9 threads) (stitch 2)

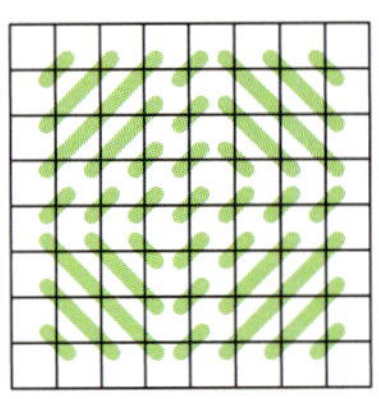

Elf Arms (30 x 20 threads)

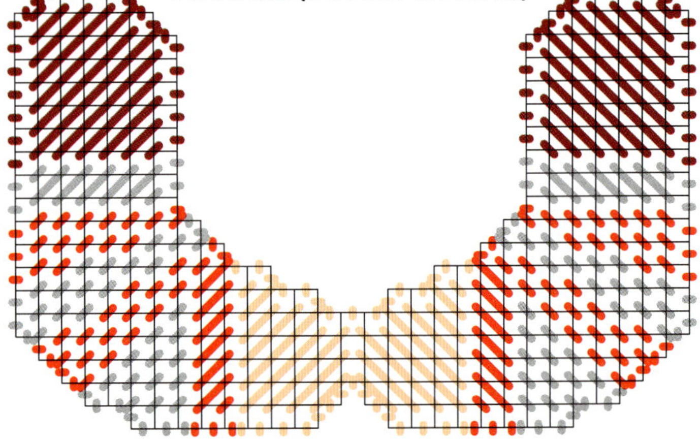

Elf Front/Back
(30 x 86 threads)
(cut 2) (stitch 1)

Left Elf Ear
(4 x 7 threads)

Right Elf Ear
(4 x 7 threads)

Elf Nose (4 x 4 threads) (cut 2)
Stack and stitch through two layers of canvas.

Elf Shoes Diagram

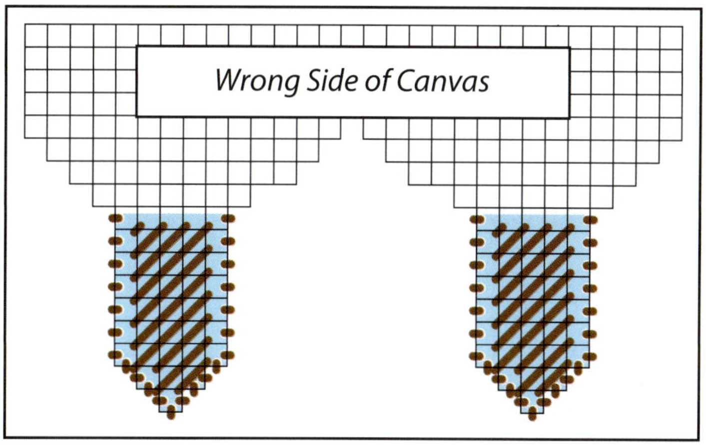

Elf Shoes (30 x 18 threads)

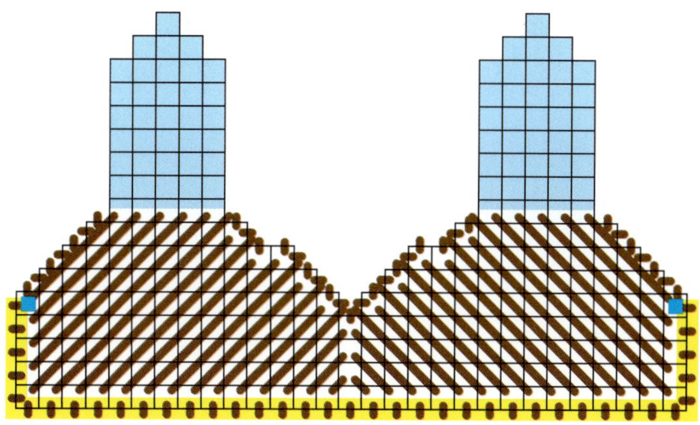

Snow Family Lineup

Design by MizFitz.

Size

20"w x 14"h

Supplies

- Six 10 1/2" x 13 1/2" sheets of 7 mesh plastic canvas
- Worsted weight yarn
- #16 tapestry needle
- Four 3" x 10" white foam board rectangles
- Thirteen assorted buttons
- Three pink silk ribbon roses
- 7" length of pre-strung pearls
- 4" x 3" cardboard rectangle
- 3" x 2" cardboard rectangle
- Craft glue

Stitches Used

Alternating Scotch Stitch, Backstitch, French Knot, Fringe, Gobelin Stitch, Overcast Stitch, and Tent Stitch

Color Key

white

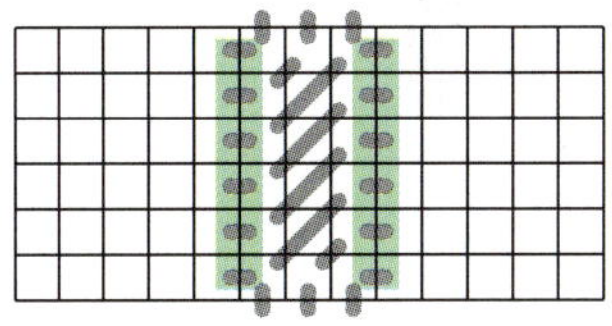

Joining the Characters

After all characters are stitched, work stitches in blue shaded areas to cover unworked edges of Fronts only. Insert Hinges in openings on piece sides. Work stitches in green shaded areas to join Hinges to unworked edges of Backs only.

Stocking Cap Snowman

Follow charts to cut and stitch pieces, leaving shaded areas unworked. Tack Eyes, edge of Nose, and Large Heart to Stocking Cap Snowman Front. Tack Scarf Tail to Scarf; tack Scarf to Stocking Cap Snowman Front. Tack Wing and Beak to Blue Bird; tack Blue Bird to Stocking Cap Snowman Front. Glue three buttons to Stocking Cap Snowman Front.

Matching ★'s, tack top and bottom edges of Hat Cuff to Stocking Cap Snowman Front. Working stitches in grey shaded areas and stitching through three layers of canvas, join Hat Cuff to Stocking Cap Snowman Front and Back.

Placing foam board rectangle between Stocking Cap Snowman Front and Back, use matching color Overcast Stitches to join unshaded edges of Stocking Cap Snowman Front and Back.

To make pom-pom for cap, cut a 5" length of red yarn. Refer to Diagrams A and B (page 63) to make the pom-pom, wrapping three yards each of blue and red yarn around 4" x 3" cardboard rectangle. Tack pom-pom to stocking cap.

Snowlady

Follow charts to cut and stitch pieces, leaving shaded areas unworked. Tack Eyes and edge of Nose to Snowlady Front. Glue ribbon roses to Earmuffs and Snowlady Front. Glue three buttons to Snowlady Front. Placing foam board rectangle between Snowlady Front and Back, use white Overcast Stitches to join unshaded edges of Snowlady Front and Back. Tack Earmuffs to Snowlady. For necklace, glue pearls in place.

Snow Girl

Follow charts to cut and stitch pieces, leaving shaded areas unworked. Tack Hat Cuff and edge of Nose to Snowgirl. Tack Scarf Knot to Scarf; tack Scarf to Snowgirl.

To make pom-pom for hat, cut a 5" length of pink yarn. Refer to Diagrams A and B (page 63) to make the pom-pom, wrapping three yards of pink yarn around 3" x 2" cardboard rectangle. Tack pom-pom to cap.

Glue Snowgirl to Snowlady Front.

Top Hat Snowman
Follow charts to cut and stitch pieces, leaving shaded areas unworked. Tack Eyes and edge of Nose to Top Hat Snowman Front. Tack Star to Hat Brim; tack Star and Hat Brim to Top Hat Snowman Front. Tack Bow to Scarf; tack Scarf to Top Hat Snowman Front. Tack Wing and Beak to Red Bird; tack Red Bird to Top Hat Snowman Front. Glue three buttons to Top Hat Snowman Front.

Placing foam board rectangle between Top Hat Snowman Front and Back, use matching color Overcast Stitches to join unshaded edges of Top Hat Snowman Front and Back.

Vested Snowman
Follow charts to cut and stitch pieces, leaving shaded areas unworked. Tack Eyes, edge of Nose and Vest pieces to Vested Snowman Front. Glue two buttons to Vested Snowman Front.

Tack Beak and Wing to Little Blue Bird; tack Little Blue Bird and Small Heart to Birdhouse. Cut a 4" length of navy yarn; glue yarn ends to wrong side of Birdhouse. Tack Birdhouse to Vested Snowman Front, looping yarn over button.

Matching ■'s, use variegated blue yarn to join Hat Brim to Hat. Matching ♥s, work stitches in pink shaded area through three layers of canvas to join Hat to Vested Snowman Front and Back.

Place foam board rectangle between Vested Snowman Front and Back. Using matching color Overcast Stitches, join unshaded edges of Vested Snowman Front and Back.

Color Key

white	lt blue
yellow	blue
orange	black
pink	black Fr. Knot
red	red fringe
purple	blue fringe

Stocking Cap Snowman Front/Back
(30 x 86 threads) (cut 2) (stitch 1)

Stocking Cap Snowman Hat Cuff (30 x 11 threads)

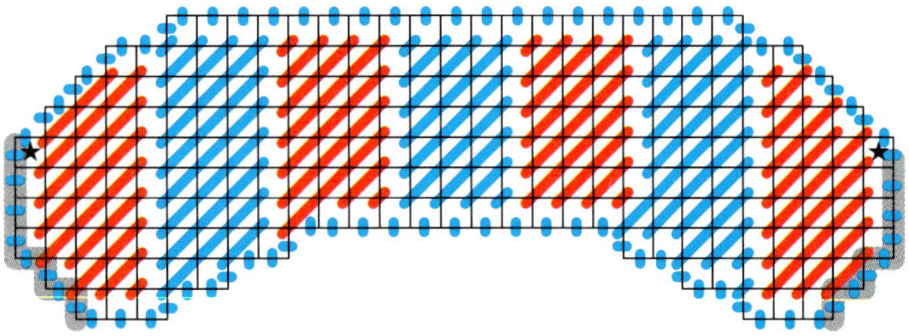

Stocking Cap Snowman Scarf (30 x 9 threads)

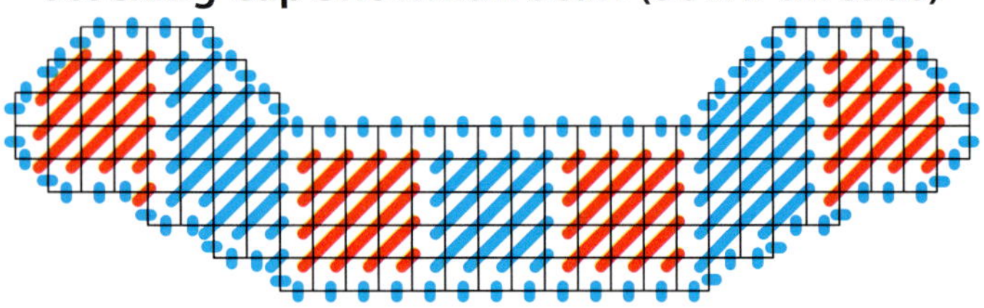

Stocking Cap Snowman Scarf Tails (15 x 13 threads)

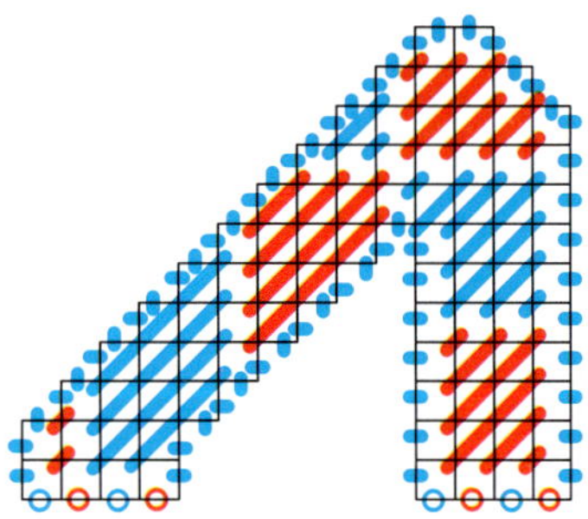

Large Heart (8 x 8 threads)

Stocking Cap
Snowman Nose
(7 x 4 threads)

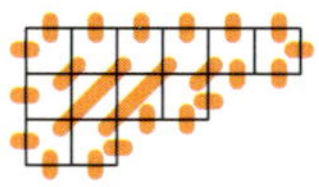

Stocking Cap
Snowman Eye
(4 x 4 threads)
(stitch 2)

Blue Bird
(17 x 17 threads)

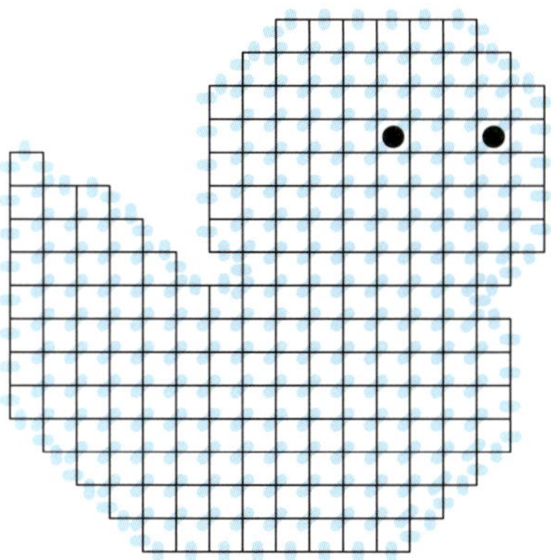

Blue Bird Wing
(11 x 6 threads)

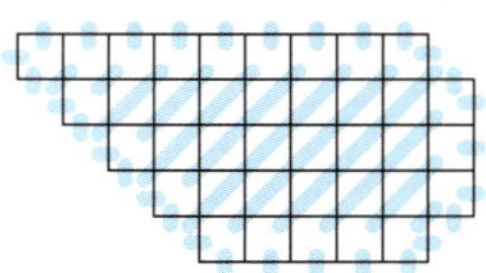

Blue Bird Beak
(4 x 4 threads)

Snowlady Front/Back
(30 x 78 threads) (cut 2) (stitch 1)

Snowlady Nose
(7 x 4 threads)

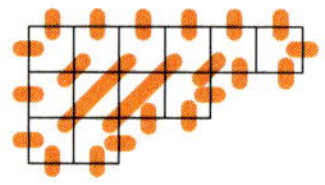

Color Key

- white
- yellow
- orange
- pink
- red
- purple
- lt green
- green
- grey
- black
- black Fr. Knot

Snowlady Earmuffs
(8 x 52 threads))

Snowgirl Scarf Tails
(9 x 12 threads)

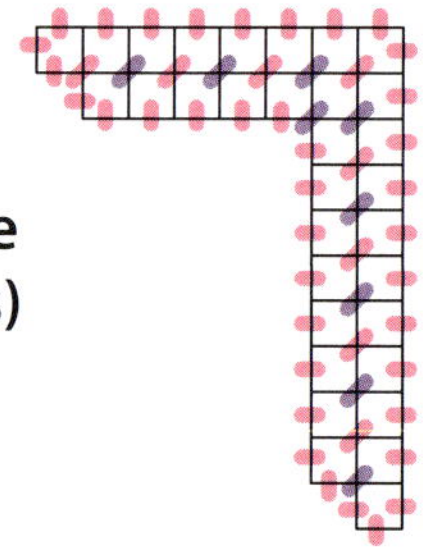

Snowlady Eye
(4 x 4 threads)
(stitch 2)

Snowgirl Scarf Knot
(4 x 4 threads)

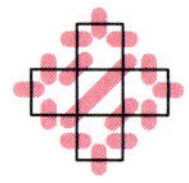

Snowgirl
(12 x 39 threads)

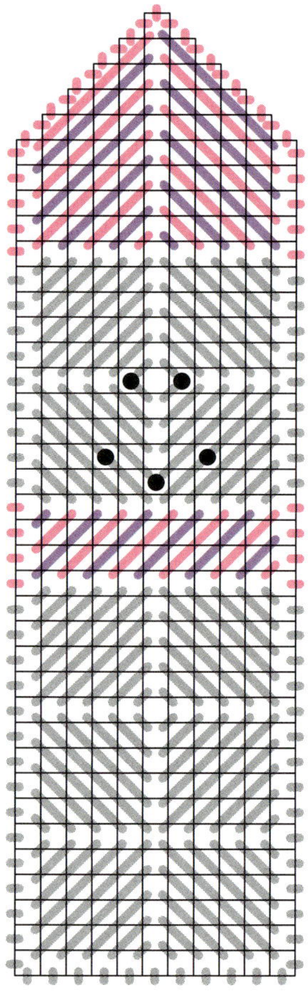

Snowgirl Nose
(5 x 3 threads)

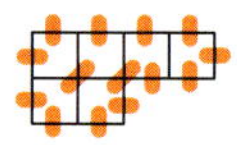

Snowgirl Hat Cuff
(13 x 4 threads)

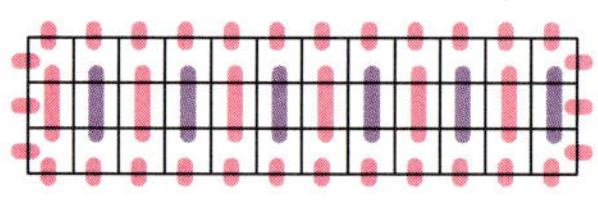

Top Hat Snowman Front/Back
(30 x 90 threads) (cut 2) (stitch 1)

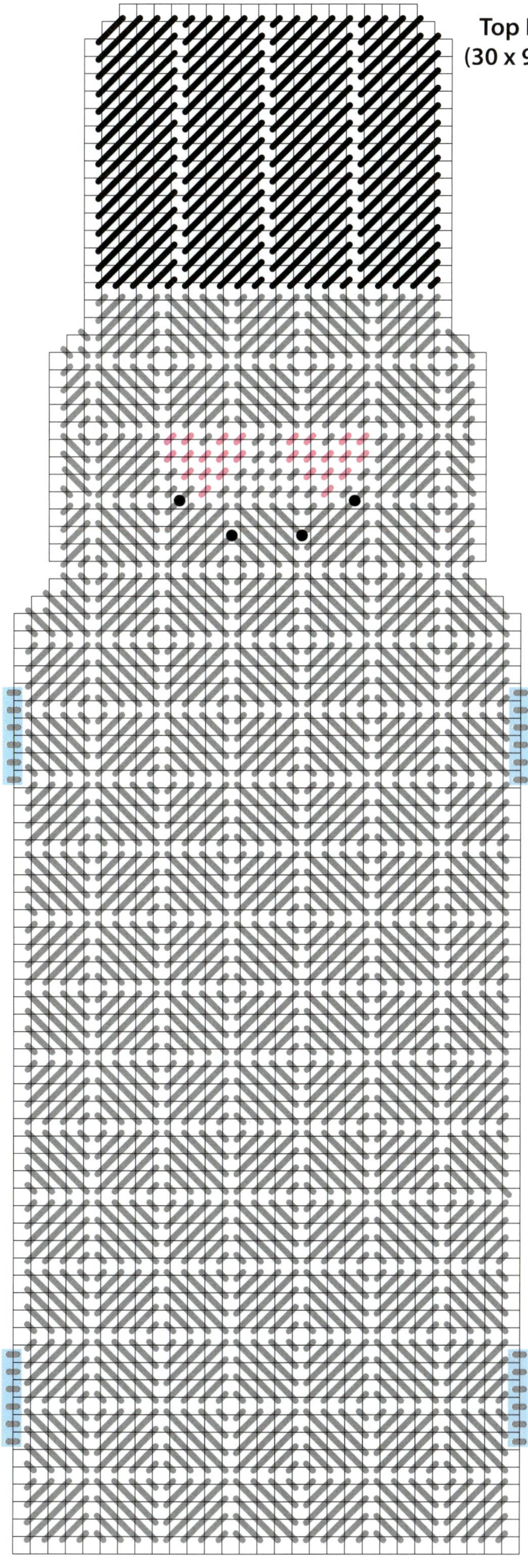

Top Hat Snowman Eye
(4 x 4 threads) (stitch 2)

Top Hat Snowman Nose
(7 x 4 threads)

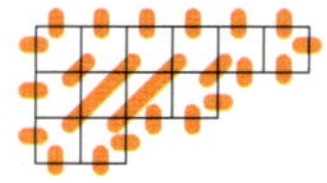

Top Hat Snowman Bow Tie
(17 x 10 threads)

Red Bird Wing
(11 x 6 threads)

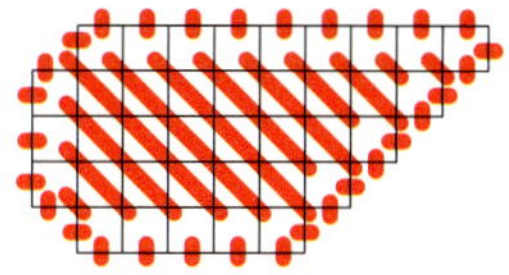

Red Bird Beak
(4 x 4 threads)

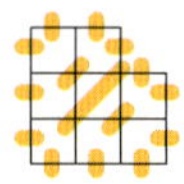

Star
(10 x 10 threads)

Red Bird
(17 x 17 threads)

Top Hat Snowman Hat Brim (32 x 7 threads)

Top Hat Snowman Scarf (30 x 9 threads)

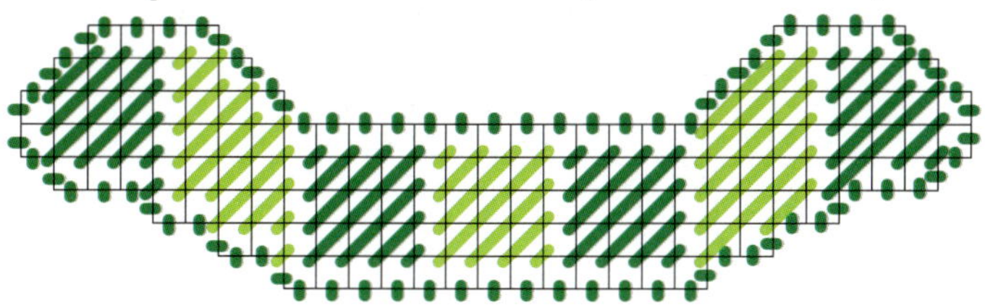

Color Key

- white
- yellow
- orange
- pink
- red
- lt blue
- variegated blue
- navy
- brown
- black
- black Fr. Knot

Vested Snowman Eye
(4 x 4 threads) (stitch 2)

Vested Snowman Nose
(7 x 4 threads)

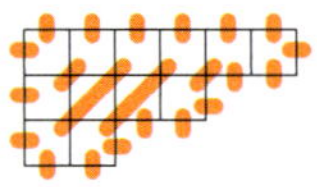

Little Blue Bird Beak
(3 x 3 threads)

Little Blue Bird
(9 x 9 threads)

Little Blue Bird Wing
(6 x 4 threads)

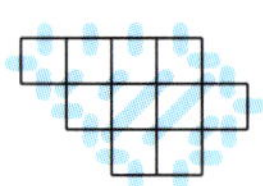

Birdhouse (20 x 24 threads)

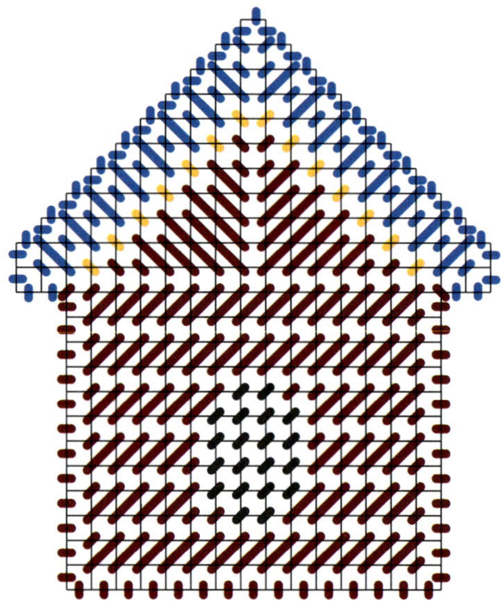

Vested Snowman Hat (26 x 15 threads)

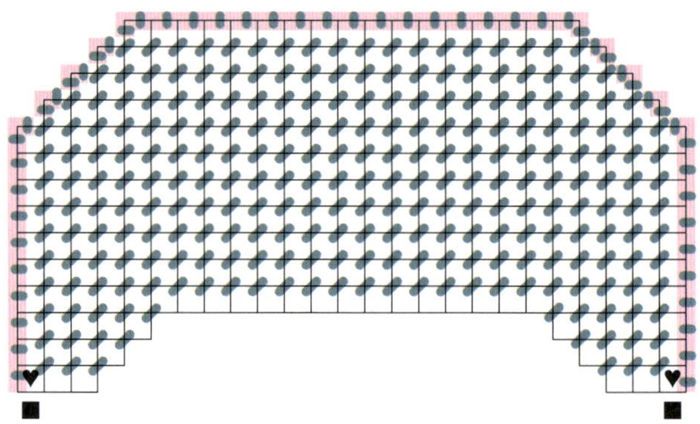

Small Heart
(6 x 5 threads)

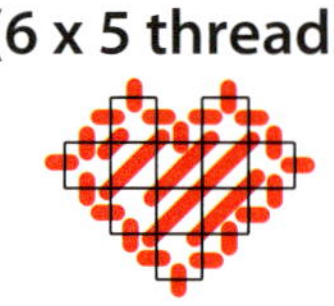

Vested Snowman Front/Back
(30 x 82 threads) (cut 2) (stitch 1)

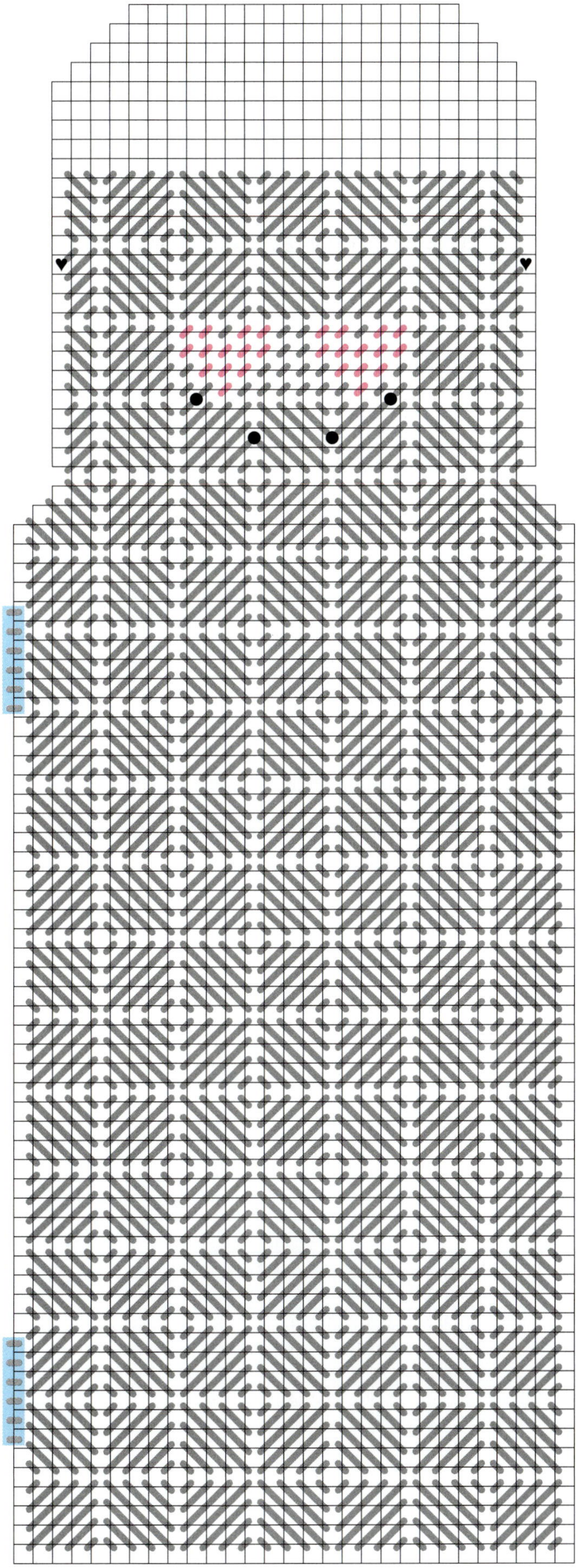

Vested Snowman Hat Brim (29 x 8 threads)

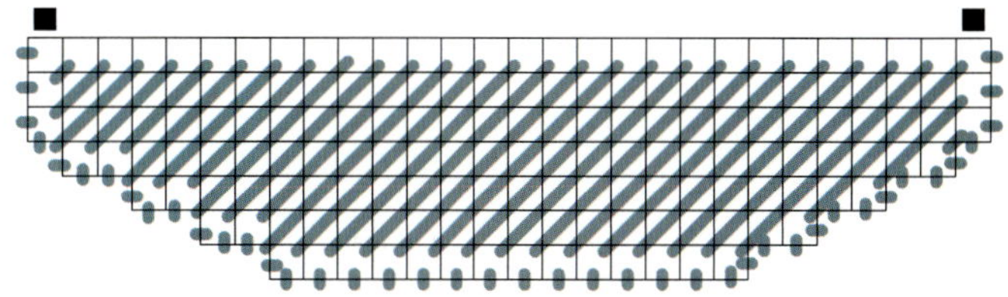

Vest Left Side
(14 x 19 threads)

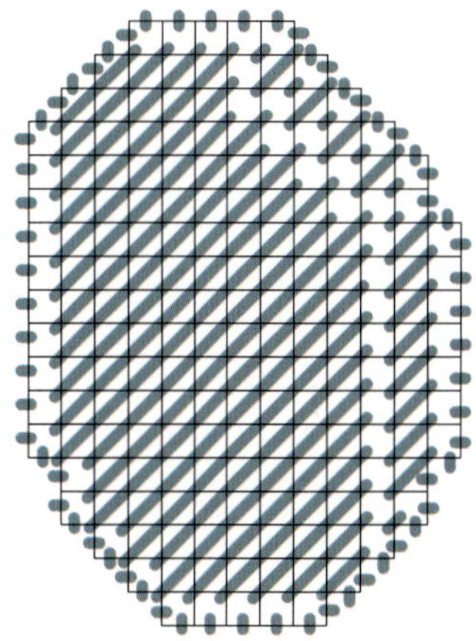

Vest Right Side
(14 x 19 threads)

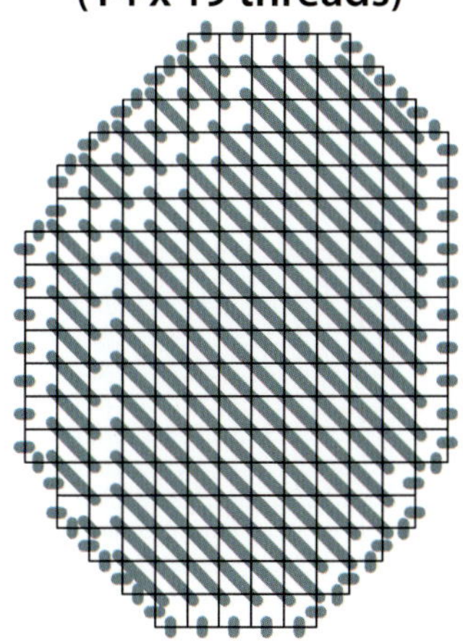

Reindeer Kiss

Size

3 1/2"w x 4 1/2"h

Supplies

One 10 1/2" x 13 1/2" sheet of 7 mesh plastic canvas
Worsted weight yarn
#16 tapestry needle

Stitches Used

Backstitch, French Knot, Gobelin Stitch, Overcast Stitch, and Tent Stitch

Instructions

Follow charts to cut and stitch Reindeer pieces. Matching ♦'s, use gold to join Top to Back along unworked threads. Matching ◒'s, use gold to join Bottom to Back along unworked threads.

Color Key

- gold
- tan
- red
- black
- dk green
- red Fr. Knot

Top (13 x 13 threads)

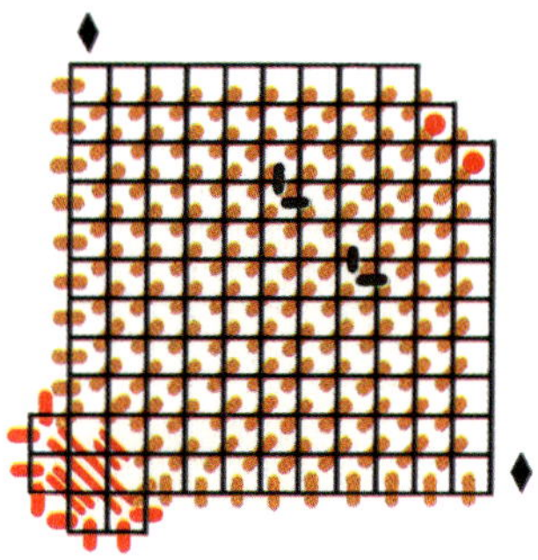

Back (30 x 30 threads)

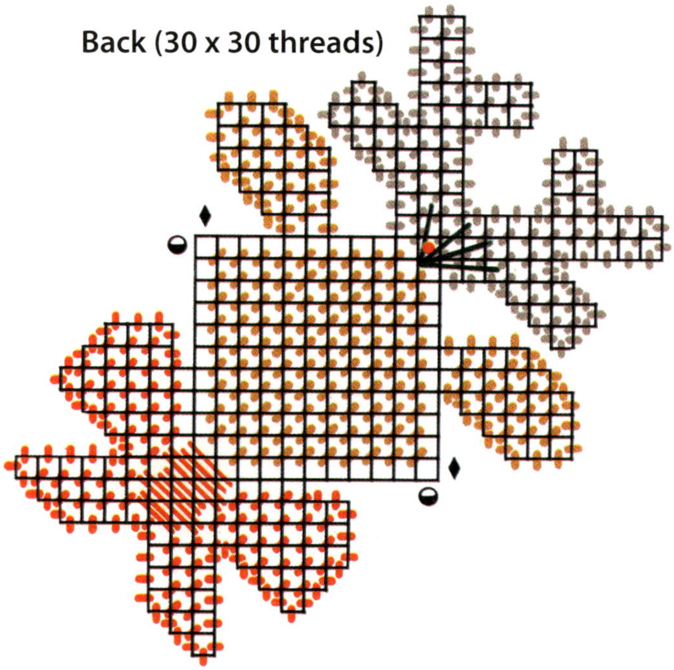

Bottom (12 x 12 threads)

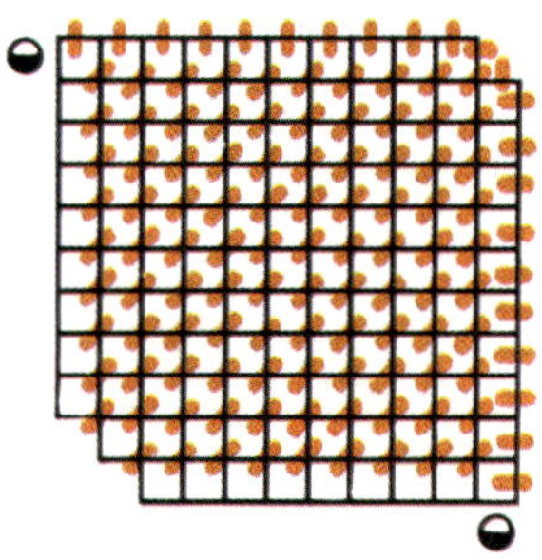

Santa Kiss

Size
3"w x 3½"h

Supplies
- One 10½" x 13½" sheet of 7 mesh plastic canvas
- Worsted weight yarn
- #16 tapestry needle

Stitches Used
Backstitch, French Knot, Fringe Stitch, Gobelin Stitch, Overcast Stitch, and Tent Stitch

Instructions
Follow charts to cut and stitch Santa pieces. Matching ♦'s, use white to join Top to Back along unworked threads. Matching ◒'s, use white to join Bottom to Back along unworked threads. Matching ★'s, use red to tack Holly to Back.

Color Key
- white
- peach
- pink
- red
- dk green
- brown
- black
- red fringe

Top (12 x 12 threads)

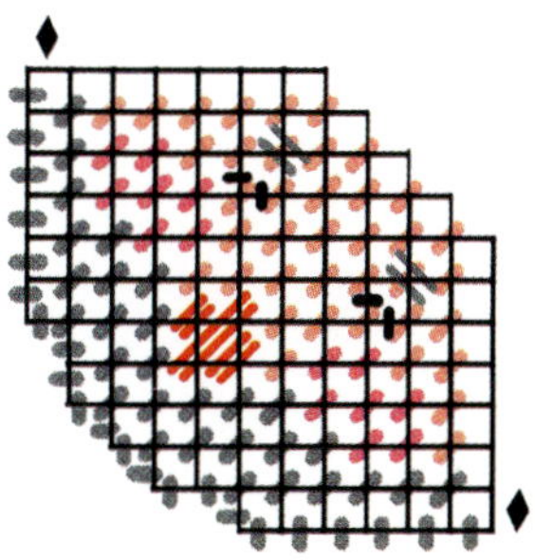

Back (20 x 23 threads)

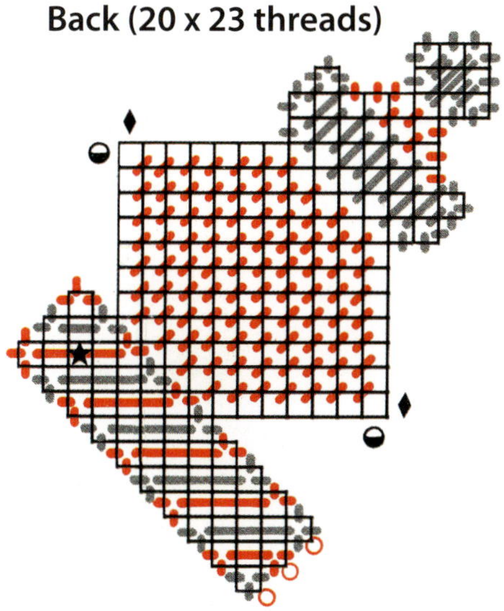

Bottom (12 x 12 threads)

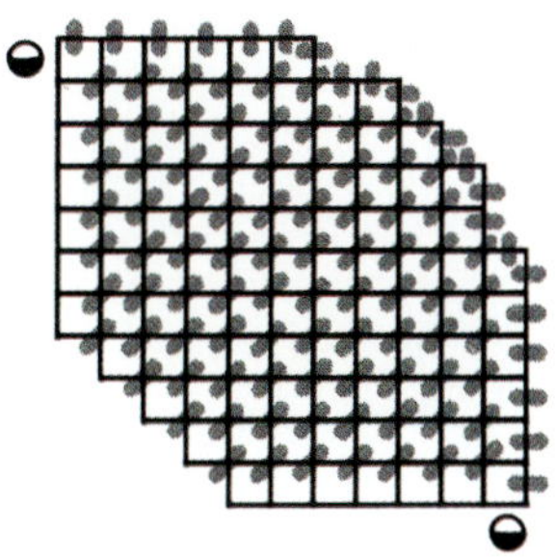

Holly (8 x 8 threads)

Candy Cane Climbers

Designs by Sandy & Honey for Studio M.

Size

approximately 2"w x 4"h each

Supplies

- 10½" x 13½" sheets of 7 mesh plastic canvas
- Medium weight yarn (refer to color keys)
- #16 tapestry needle
- Cloth-covered floral wire (see project instructions for colors and amounts)
- Two 8mm wiggle eyes (for each project)
- 5mm red pom-poms
- 8" length of ¼"w red satin ribbon (for each project except Santa)
- Craft glue
- ***For Clown only:*** ½" red pom-pom
- ***For Mouse only:*** 5mm pink pom-pom
- ***For Santa only:*** ¼" white pom-pom

To make each Climber:

Follow charts to cut out and use required stitches to work Candy Cane Climber pieces. Referring to the photos and instructions below, use Overcast Stitches to join the pieces. After the Climber is assembled, tie ribbon into a bow and trim ends. Glue the bow to the Climber. Glue Leaf, wiggle eyes and pom-poms to Climber.

Cat

For Back, turn unworked Front over and work with white Tent Stitches. With wrong sides together, join Front to Back. Refer to photo to shape 2½" of black cloth-covered floral wire. Glue black floral wire to Front. Glue Arms to Front and Back. Glue short ends of Arms together. Glue Legs to Front and Back. For tail, cut three 10" lengths of white yarn, one 10" length of white cloth-covered floral wire, one 8" length of white yarn and one 8" length of red yarn. Fold 10" yarn lengths and white floral wire in half together. Secure fold with 8" white yarn length. Braid white yarn and wire together for 3". Tie red yarn in a bow around braid end. Glue tail to Back and trim ends.

Clown

With wrong sides together, join Front to Back. Refer to photo to shape 1¾" of black cloth-covered floral wire. Glue wire to Front. Glue Arms to Front and Back. Glue short ends of Arms together. Glue Legs to Front and Back. Make two 1" red pom-poms (page 63), using a 1" x 2" cardboard rectangle. Glue these pom-poms to Front.

Cow

With wrong sides together, join Front to Back. Glue Muzzle to Front. Refer to photo to shape 1½" of black cloth-covered floral wire. Glue wire to Muzzle. Glue Arms to Front and Back. Glue short ends of Arms together. Glue Legs to Front and Back. For tail, cut three 10" lengths of white yarn, one 8" length of red yarn, and two 6" lengths of black yarn. Knot the black yarn lengths together in the center; trim ends to ½". Knot white yarn lengths close to one end. Braid yarn for 2". Tie red yarn in a bow around braid end; trim ends of yarn. Glue knotted black yarn to end of braid. Glue tail to Back.

Dog

With wrong sides together, join Front to Back. Glue Muzzle and Ears to Front. Glue Arms to Front and Back. Glue short ends of Arms together. Glue Legs to Front and Back.

Mouse

For Back, turn unworked Front over and work with grey Tent Stitches. With wrong sides together, join Front to Back. Glue two 2" lengths of black cloth-covered floral wire to the wrong side of Nose. Glue Nose to Front. Glue Arms to Front and Back. Glue short ends of Arms together. Glue Legs to Front and Back. For tail, cut three 10" lengths of grey yarn and one 8" length of pink yarn. Knot grey yarn lengths together close to one end. Braid yarn for $2^{1}/_{4}$". Tie pink yarn in a bow around braid end. Glue tail to Back and trim ends.

Pig

For Back, turn unworked Front over and work with pink Tent Stitches. With wrong sides together, join Front to Back. Glue Snout to Front. Glue Arms to Front and Back. Glue short ends of Arms together. Glue Legs to Front and Back. For tail, cut three 10" lengths of pink yarn, 10" length of pink cloth-covered floral wire and one 8" length of red yarn. Knot pink yarn lengths and wire together close to one end. Braid yarn and wire together for $2^{1}/_{4}$". Tie red yarn in a bow around braid end. Glue tail to Back and trim ends. To curl, wrap braided area around a pencil.

Polar Bear

For Back, turn unworked Front over and work with white Tent Stitches. With wrong sides together, join Front to Back. Glue Muzzle to Front.Glue Arms to Front and Back. Glue short ends of Arms together. Glue Legs to Front and Back.

Reindeer

With wrong sides together, join Front to Back. Glue Muzzle to Front. Glue Arms to Front and Back. Glue short ends of Arms together. Glue Legs to Front and Back.

Snowman

With wrong sides together, join Front to Back. Glue Nose to Front. Glue Brim to Front. Glue Arms to Front and Back. Glue short ends of Arms together. Glue Legs to Front and Back.

Santa

With wrong sides together, join Front to Back. Glue Beard to Front. Glue Arms to Front and Back. Glue short ends of Arms together. Glue Legs to Front and Back.

Teddy Bear

With wrong sides together, join Front to Back. Glue Muzzle to Front. Glue Arms to Front and Back. Glue short ends of Arms together. Glue Legs to Front and Back.

Toad

Use orange to work Bullion Knot on Front between 1 and 2. With wrong sides together, join Front to Back. Refer to photo and shape $1^{1}/_{4}$" length of black cloth-covered floral wire. Glue Legs to Front and Back. Glue short ends of upper Legs together.

TEDDY BEAR

Color Key
- red
- green
- lt brown
- brown

Arm (12 x 5 threads) (work 2)

Front
(12 x 22 threads)

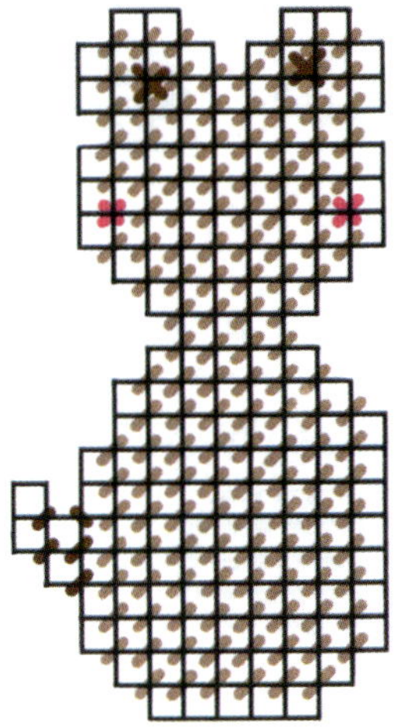

Back
(12 x 22 threads)

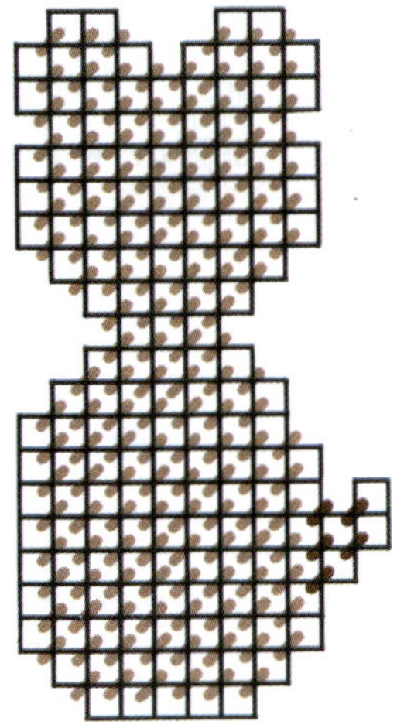

Leaf (6 x 4 threads)

Muzzle (6 x 5 threads)

Leg A
(7 x 12 threads)

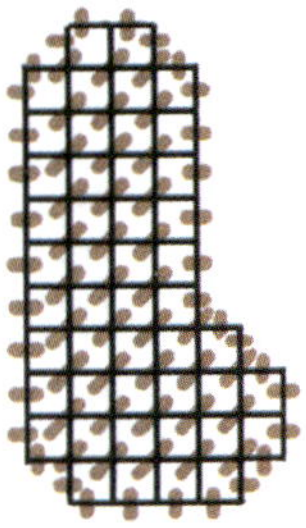

Leg B
(7 x 12 threads)

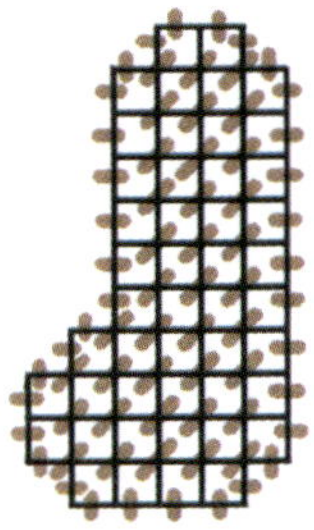

CLOWN

Color Key
- white
- yellow
- red
- lt green
- green

Front
(9 x 25 threads)

Back
(9 x 25 threads)

Leaf (6 x 4 threads)

Arm (12 x 5 threads)
(work 2)

Leg A
(7 x 12 threads)

Leg B
(7 x 12 threads)

CAT

Color Key
- white
- red
- green

Leaf (6 x 4 threads)

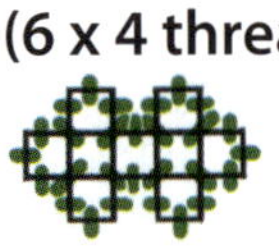

Arm (5 x 12 threads)
(stitch 2)

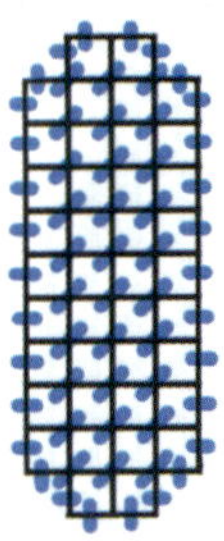

Leg A
(7 x 12 threads)

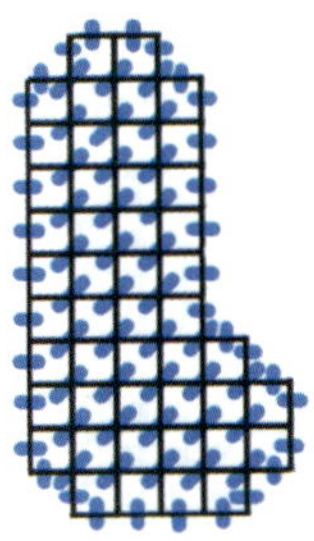

Leg B
(7 x 12 threads)

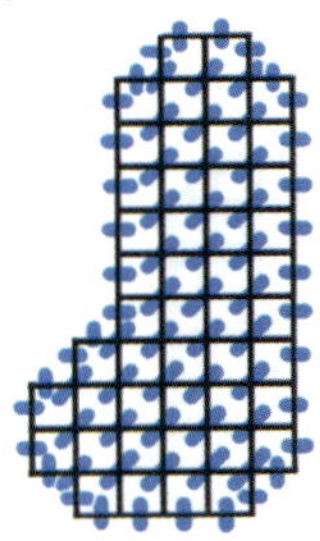

Front/Back
(10 x 22 threads)
(cut 2, stitch 1)

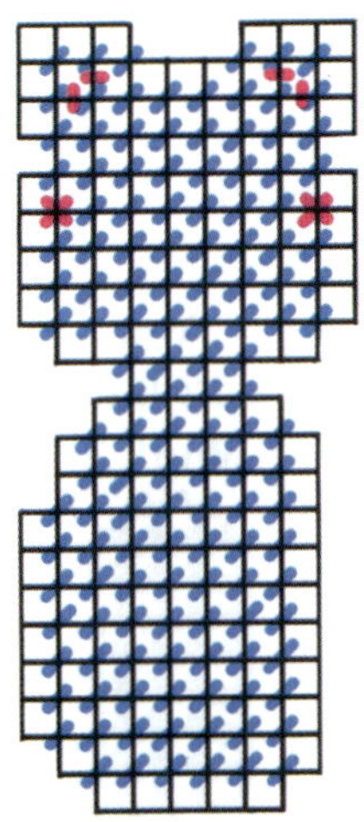

COW

Color Key
- white
- yellow
- green
- black
- red Fr. Knot

Front (16 x 23 threads)

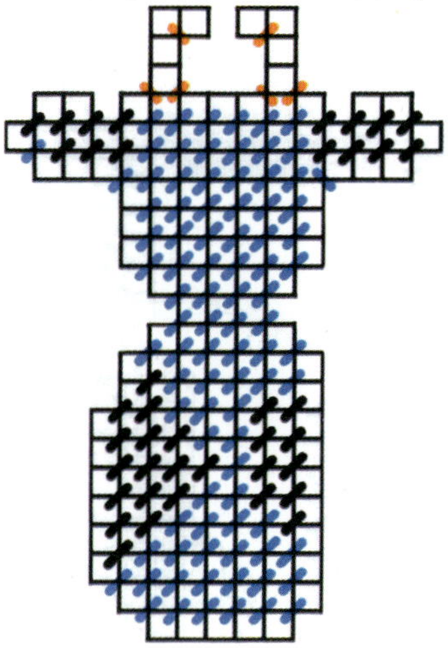

Back (16 x 23 threads)

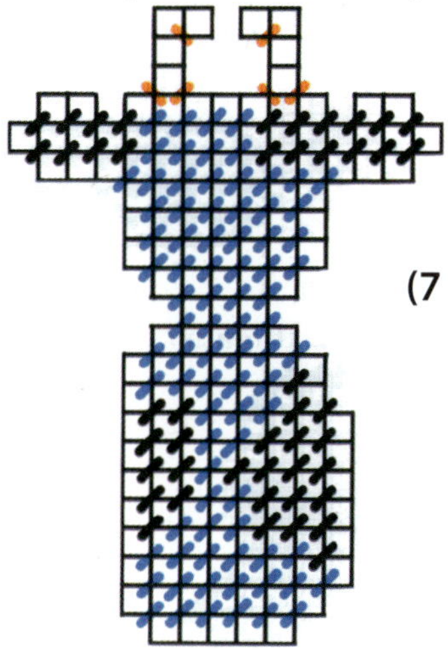

Arm (12 x 5 threads) (work 2)

Leaf (6 x 4 threads)

Muzzle (6 x 5 threads)

Leg A (7 x 12 threads)

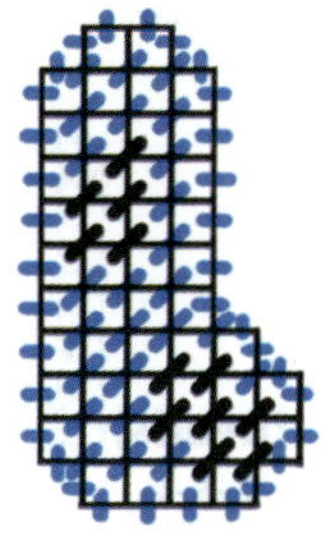

Leg B (7 x 12 threads)

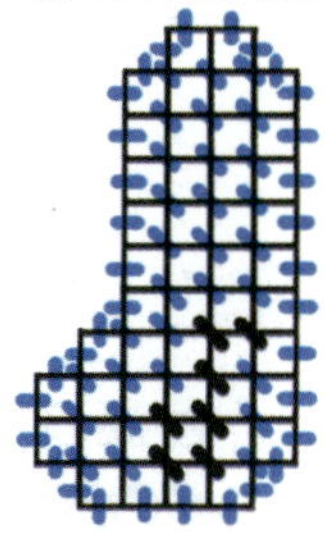

MOUSE

Color Key
- pink
- green
- grey

Nose (5 x 5 threads)

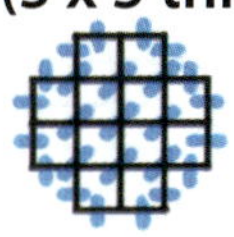

Leaf (6 x 4 threads)

Arm (5 x 12 threads) (work 2)

Leg A (7 x 12 threads)

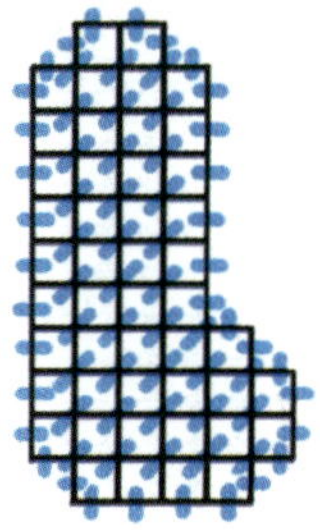

Leg B (7 x 12 threads)

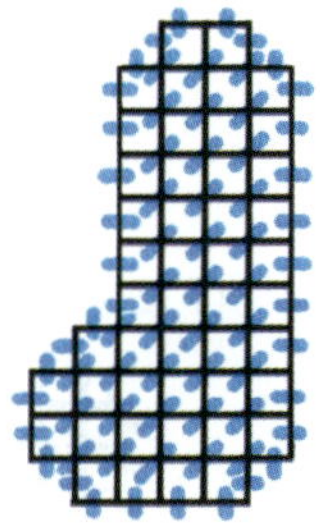

Front/Back (15 x 23 threads) (cut 2, stitch 1)

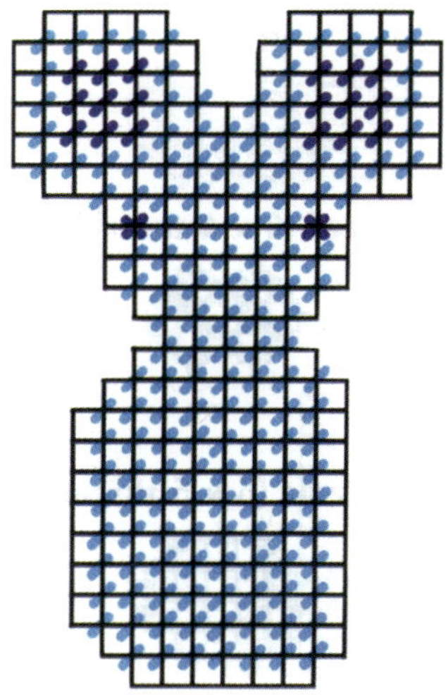

DOG

Color Key
- green
- lt brown
- brown

Muzzle (6 x 5 threads)

Leaf (6 x 4 threads)

Ear A (8 x 9 threads)

Ear B (8 x 9 threads)

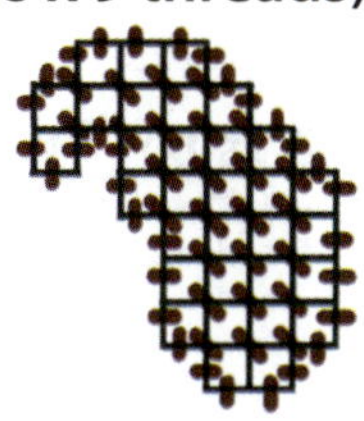

Arm (5 x 12 threads) (work 2)

Front (13 x 21 threads)

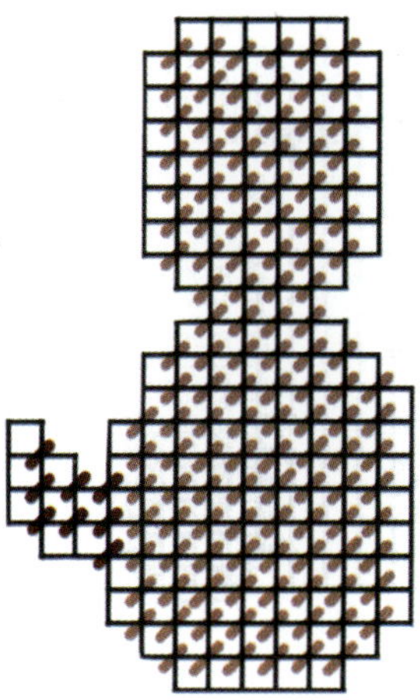

Back (13 x 21 threads)

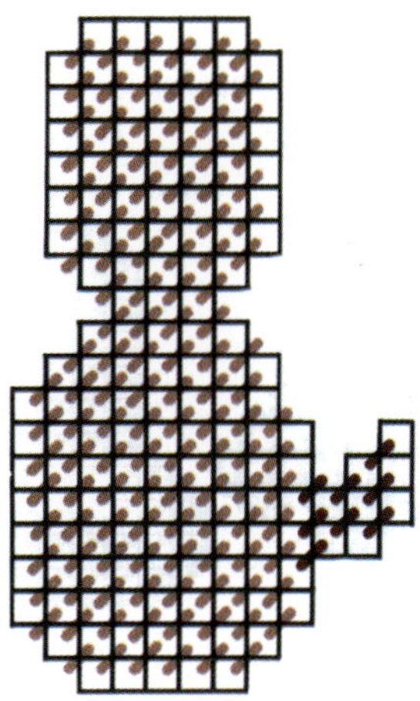

Leg A (7 x 12 threads)

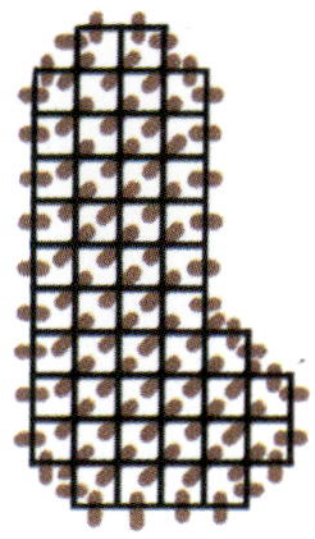

Leg B (7 x 12 threads)

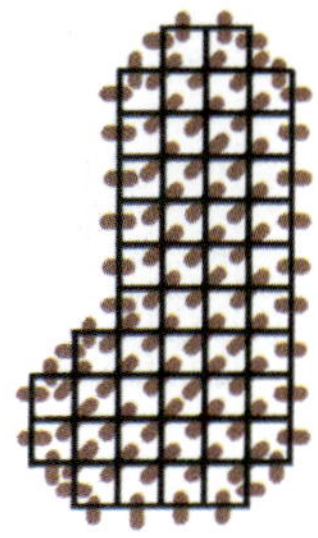

SNOWMAN

Color Key
- white
- red
- green
- black
- black Fr. Knot

Nose (4 x 4 threads)

Arm (12 x 5 threads) (work 2)

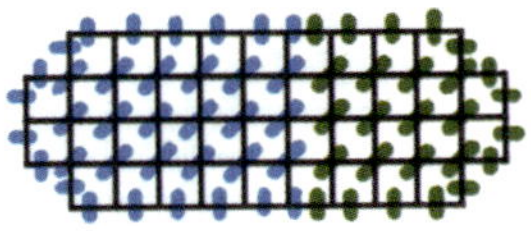

Front (10 x 24 threads)

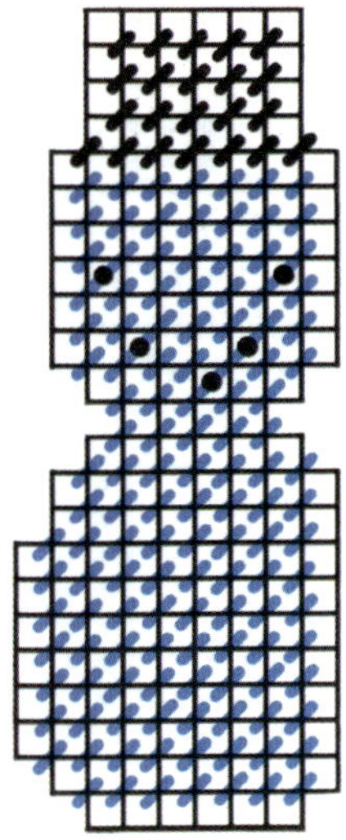

Back (10 x 24 threads)

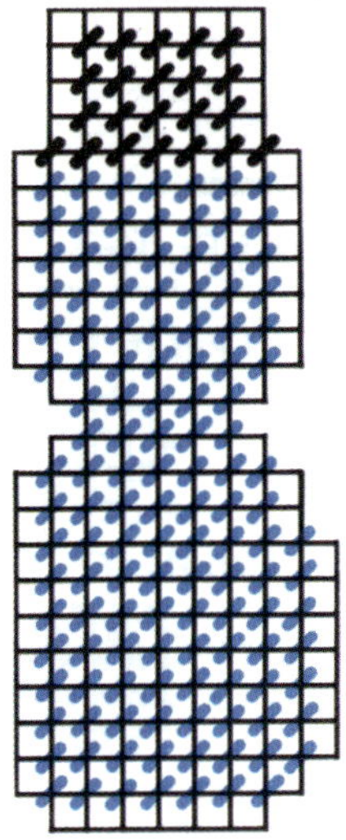

Leaf (6 x 4 threads) (stitch 2)

Leg A (7 x 12 threads)

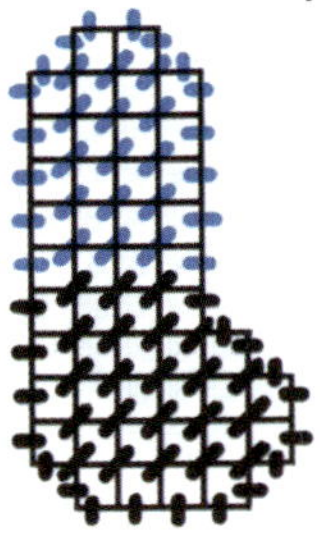

Leg B (7 x 12 threads)

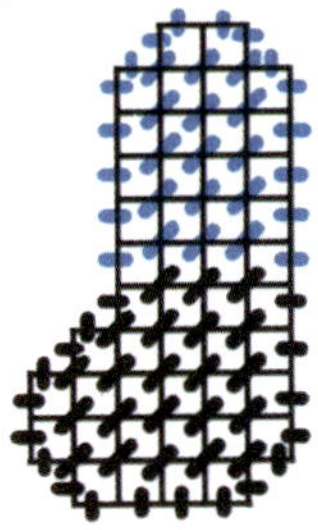

Brim (12 x 3 threads)

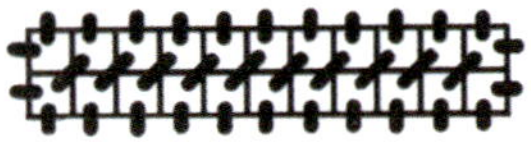

POLAR BEAR

Color Key
- white
- red
- green

Arm (12 x 5 threads) (work 2)

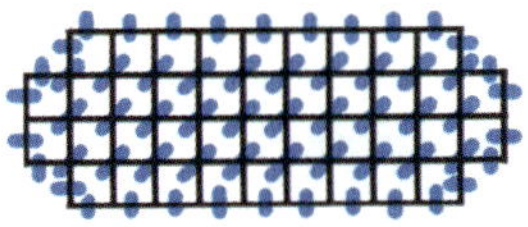

Front/Back (12 x 22 threads) (cut 2, stitch 1)

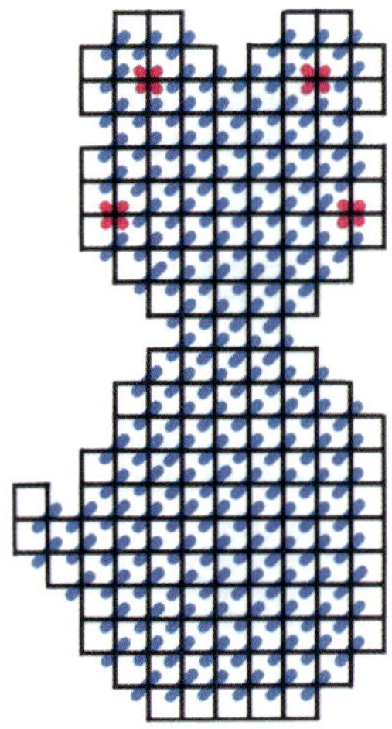

Leaf (6 x 4 threads)

Leg A (7 x 12 threads)

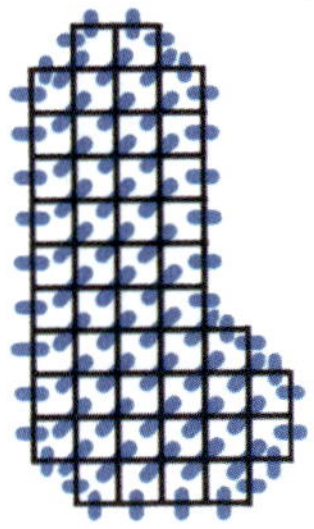

Leg B (7 x 12 threads)

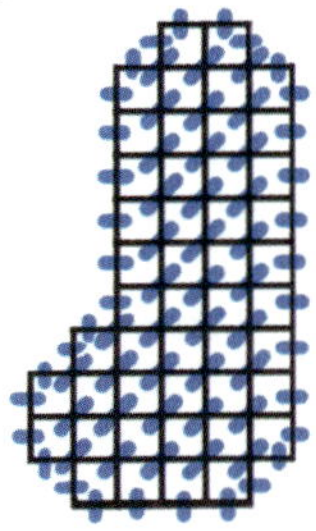

Muzzle (6 x 5 threads)

TOAD

Color Key
- lt green
- green
- yellow Fr. Knot

Front (12 x 21 threads)

Back (12 x 21 threads)

Leg (9 x 12 threads) (stitch 4)

Leaf (6 x 4 threads)

PIG

Color Key
- pink
- dk pink
- green
- dk pink Fr. Knot

Leaf (6 x 4 threads)

Snout (6 x 5 threads)

Front/Back (10 x 22 threads)
(cut 2, stitch 1)

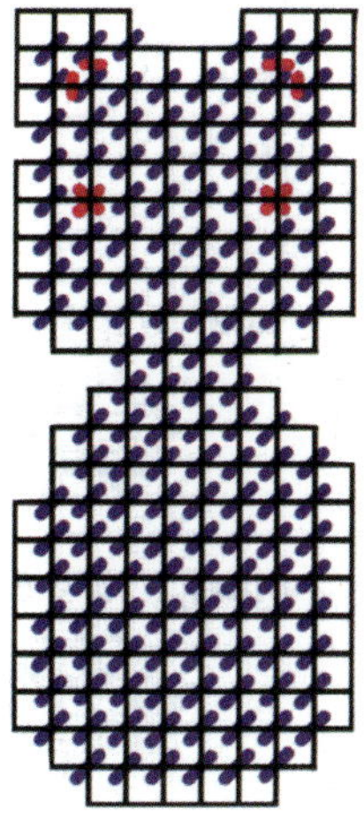

Leg A
(7 x 12 threads)

Leg B
(7 x 12 threads)

Arm (12 x 5 threads) (work 2)

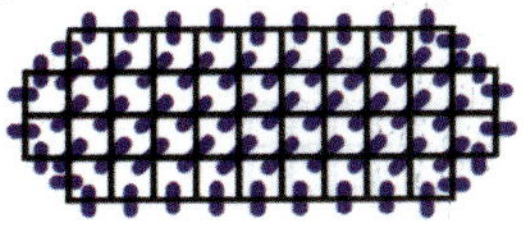

REINDEER

Color Key
- yellow
- green
- lt brown
- brown

Arm (12 x 5 threads)
(work 2)

Front (16 x 24 threads)

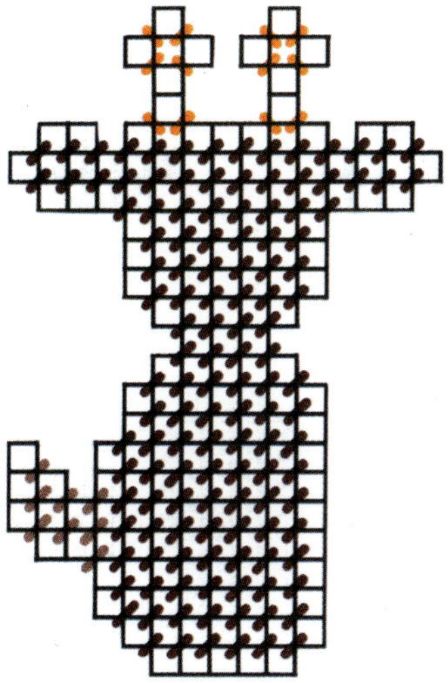

Back (16 x 24 threads)

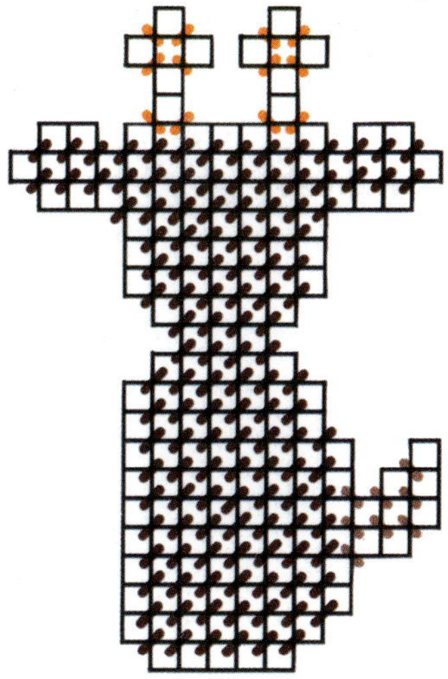

Muzzle (6 x 5 threads)

Leg A
(7 x 11 threads)

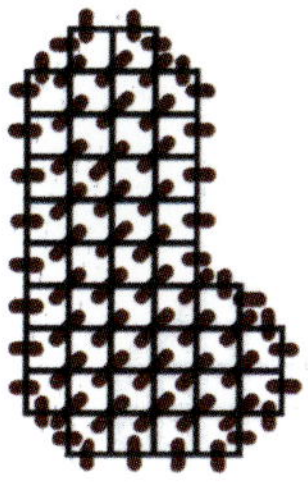

Leg B
(7 x 11 threads)

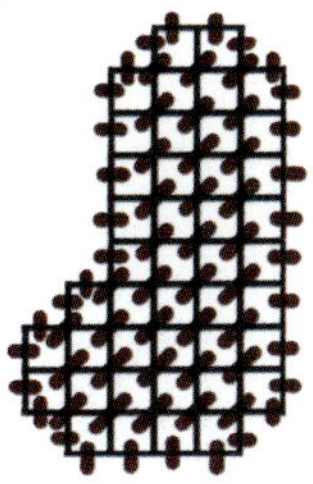

Leaf (6 x 4 threads)

SANTA

Color Key
- white
- yellow
- pink
- red
- green
- black

Leaf
(6 x 4 threads)
(stitch 2)

Beard
(11 x 9 threads)

Front
(9 x 25 threads)

Back
(9 x 25 threads)

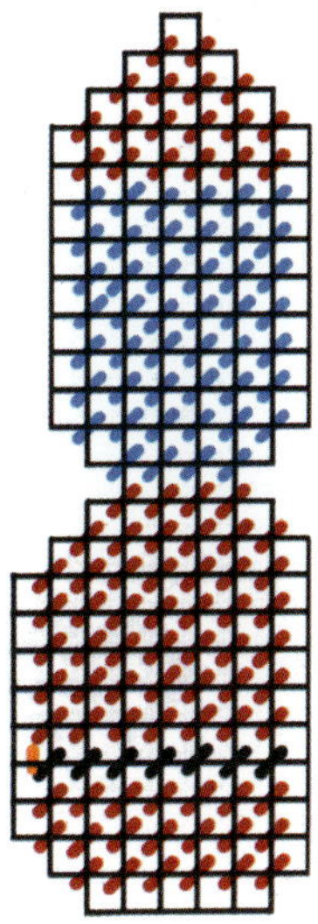

Arm (12 x 5 threads)
(work 2)

Leg A
(7 x 11 threads)

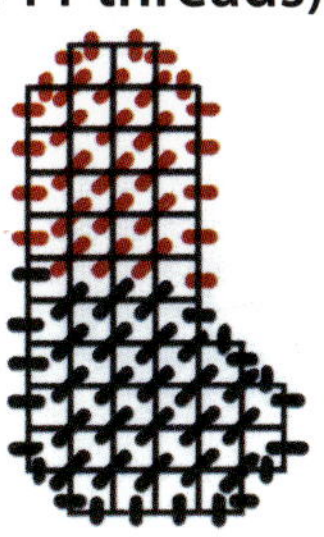

Leg B
(7 x 11 threads)

Holiday Magnets

Designs by Dick Martin.

Size

approximately $2^{3}/_{4}$"w x 3"h each

Supplies

$10^{1}/_{2}$" x $13^{1}/_{2}$" sheets of 7 mesh plastic canvas
Medium weight yarn
Kreinik heavy (#32) metallic gold braid
#16 tapestry needle
Magnetic strip
Craft glue

To make each Magnet:

Follow charts to cut out and use required stitches to work Magnet pieces. Trim magnetic strip to desired size and glue to back of stitched piece.

Mice tails

Cut a 6" length of grey yarn. Knot the yarn close to one end. Refer to the photo to glue the knotted end to the Front of the magnet. Secure the loose yarn end on the wrong side of the magnet.

Bell

Cut an 8" length of red yarn. Tie the yarn in a bow and trim the ends. Glue the bow to the bell.

Snowman

Cut an 8" length of purple yarn. Tie yarn around Snowman and trim ends.

Wagon Mouse

Match ✱'s and use green Overcast Stitches to join Arm to Wagon Mouse. For scarf, cut an 8" length of red yarn. Tie yarn around Wagon Mouse and trim ends.

Color Key

white	lt blue	metallic gold
yellow	blue	metallic gold - 2 strands
peach	lt green	metallic gold Fr. Knot
gold	green	white Fr. Knot
dk gold	green 2-ply	pink 2-ply Fr. Knot
orange 2-ply	beige	red Fr. Knot
lt pink	tan	green Fr. Knot
pink	brown	black Fr. Knot
red	grey	green 2-ply Turkey Loop
red 2-ply	black	
purple	black 2-ply	

Wagon Mouse
(22 x 23 threads)

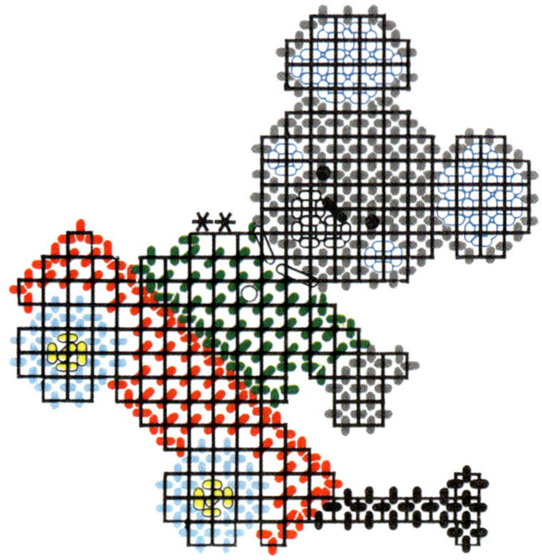

Arm
(7 x 4 threads)

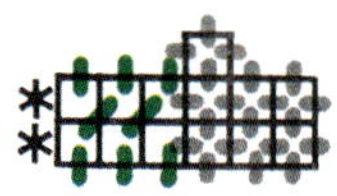

Bell
(16 x 16 threads)

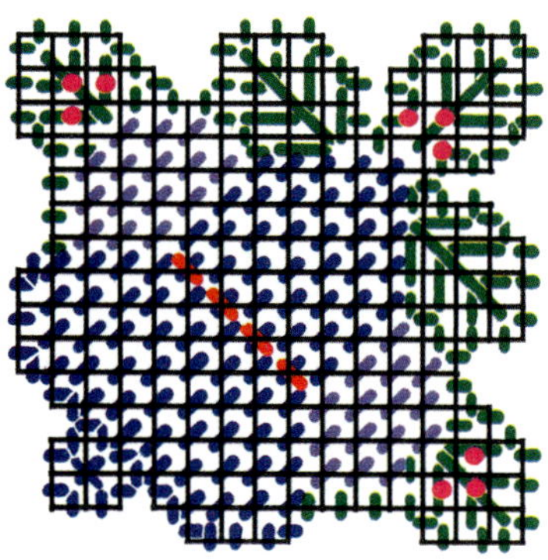

Santa
(17 x 18 threads)

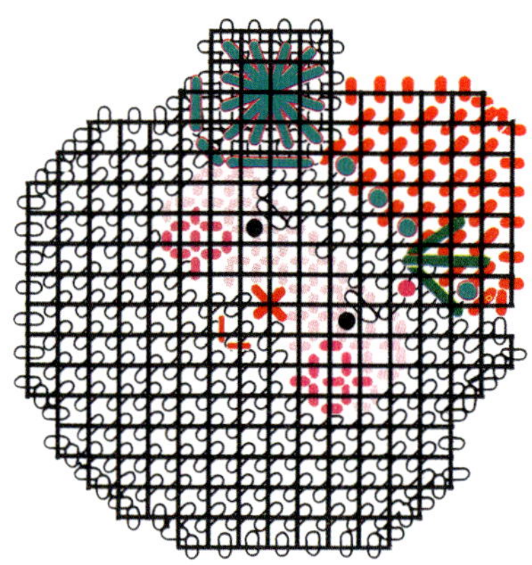

Candle
(17 x 16 threads)

Dog
(21 x 21 threads)

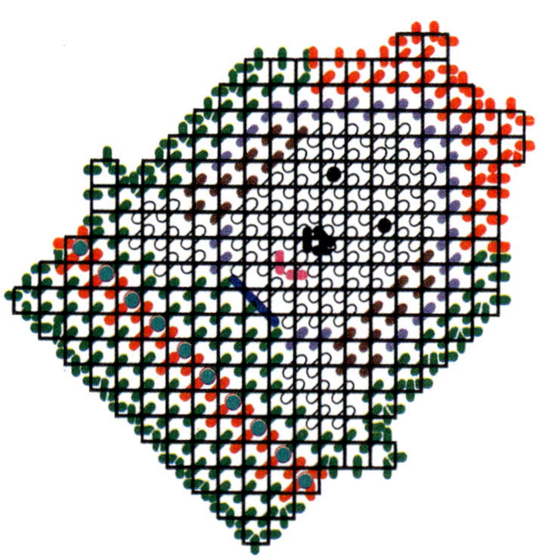

Angel
(17 x 17 threads)

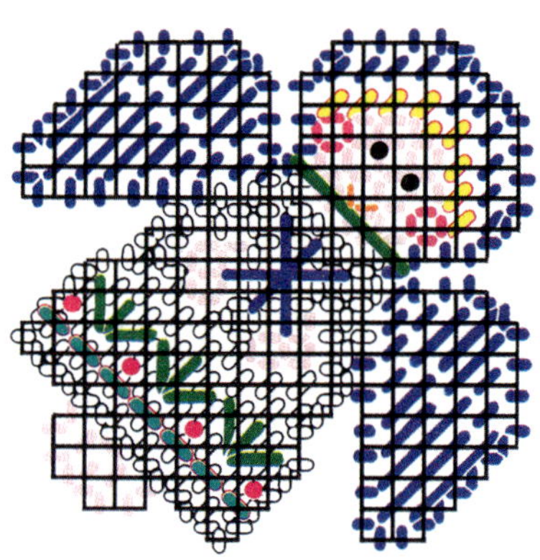

Cat
(19 x 21 threads)

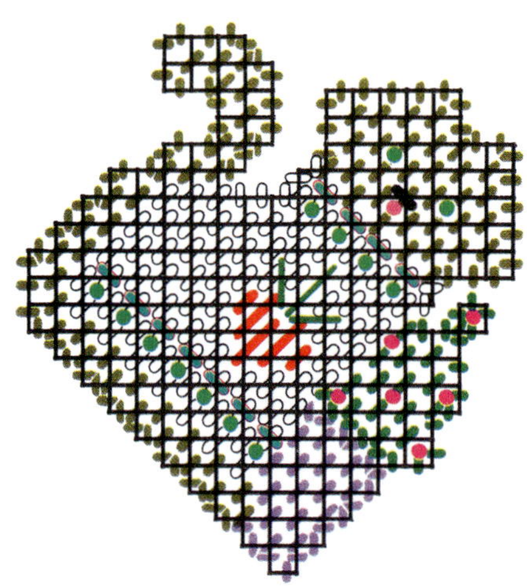

Mrs. Mouse
(22 x 22 threads)

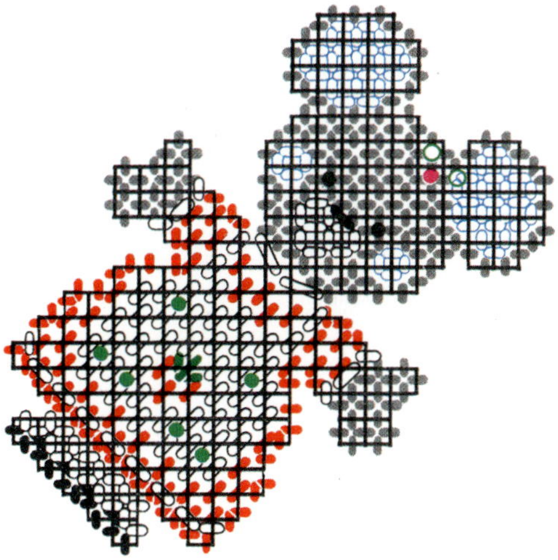

Santa Mouse
(23 x 27 threads)

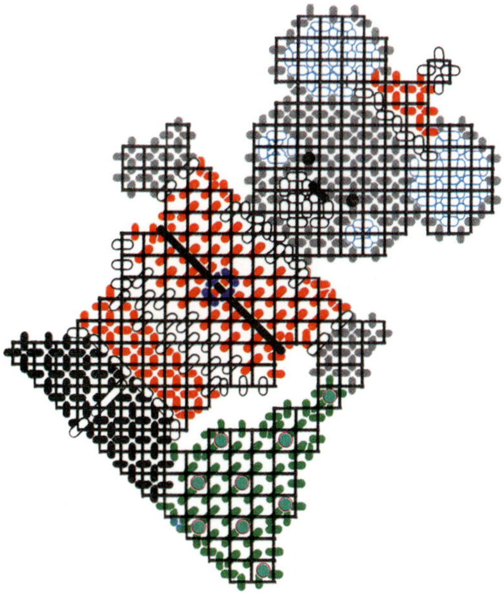

Angel Mouse
(22 x 22 threads)

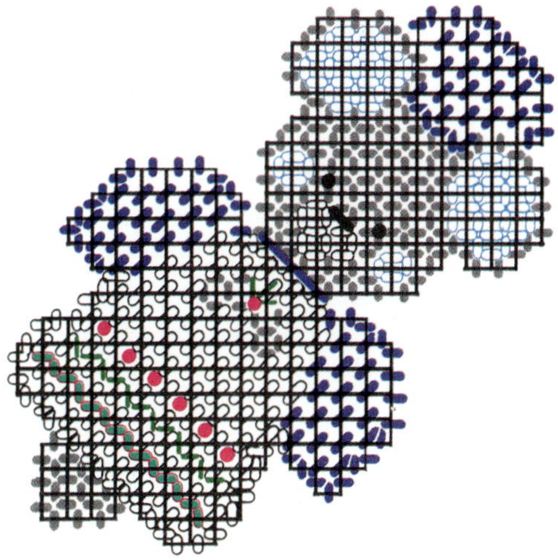

Horn
(19 x 19 threads)

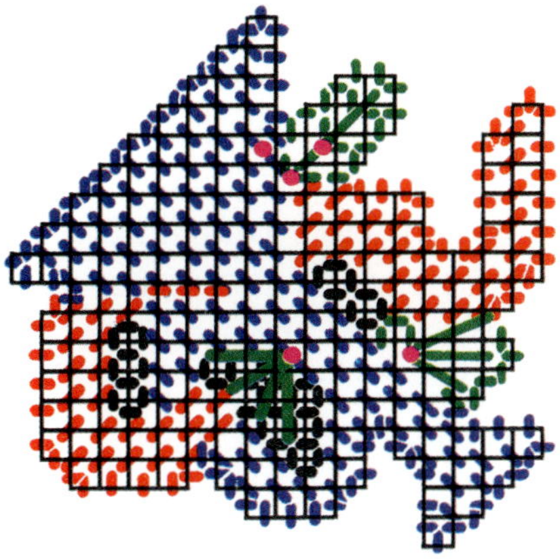

Bear
(21 x 21 threads)

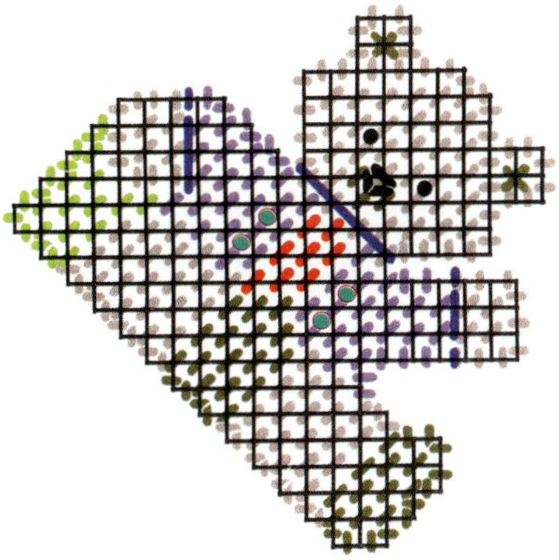

Dove
(18 x 18 threads)

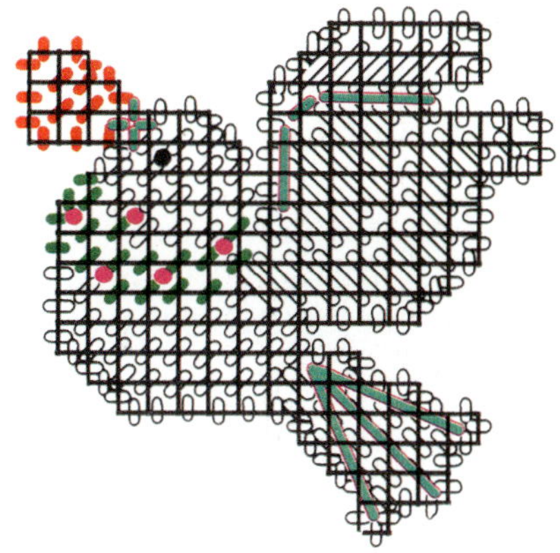

Nutcracker
(22 x 21 threads)

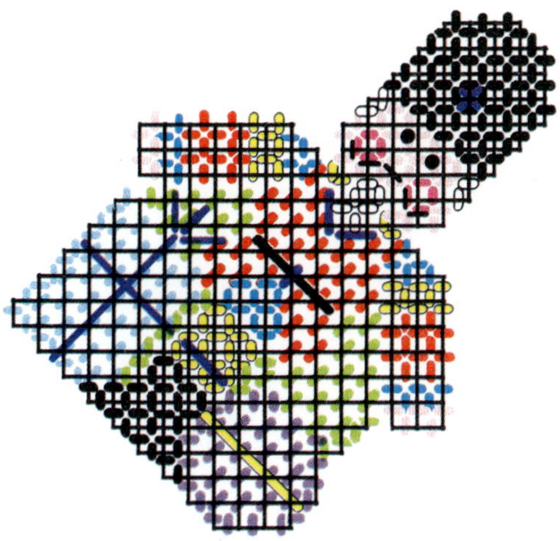

Snowman
(16 x 16 threads)

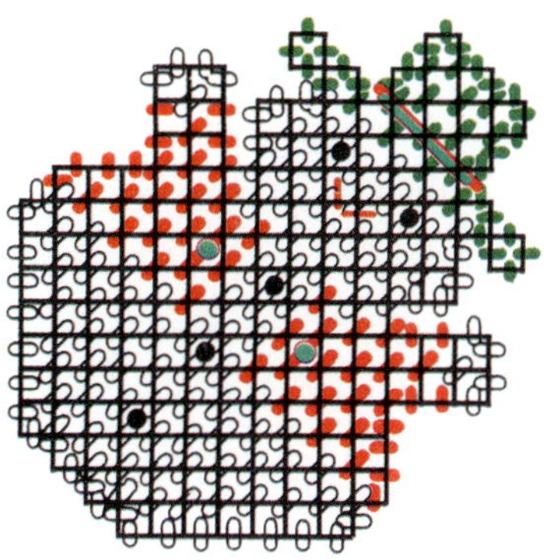

Train
(24 x 21 threads)

General Instructions

Working with Plastic Canvas

Counting Threads. The lines of the canvas are referred to as threads. Before cutting out the pieces, note the thread count of each chart listed above the chart, indicating the number of threads in the width and height. To cut plastic canvas pieces accurately, count **threads** (not **holes**) as shown in **Fig. 1**.

Fig. 1

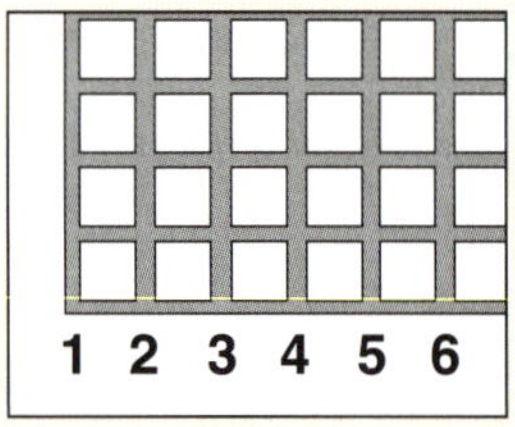

Marking the Canvas. You may use an overhead projector pen to mark the canvas. Outline shape with pen, cut out shape, and remove markings before stitching.

Cutting the Canvas. Cut as close to the thread as possible without cutting into the thread. If you don't cut close enough, "nubs" or "pickets" will be left on the edge. Make sure to cut all nubs from the canvas before stitching because nubs will snag the yarn and are difficult to cover. A craft knife is helpful when cutting a small area from the center of a larger piece of canvas. When using a craft knife, protect the table below with a layer of cardboard.

When cutting canvas along a diagonal, cut through the center of each intersection. This will leave enough plastic canvas on both sides of the cut so that both pieces may be used. Properly cut diagonal corners will be less likely to snag yarn and are easier to cover.

Working with Yarn

Most brands of medium weight yarn have plies which are twisted together to form one strand. When the instructions indicate two plies of yarn, separate the strand of yarn and stitch using only two of the plies.

Reading the Color Key

A color key is included for each project, indicating the color used for each stitch on the chart. Additional information may also be included, such as the number of plies to use when working a particular stitch.

Reading the Chart

When possible, the drawing on the chart looks like the completed stitch. For example, the tent stitches on the chart are drawn diagonally across an intersection of threads just as they look on the piece. When a stitch cannot be clearly drawn on the chart, like a French Knot, a symbol will be used instead.

Stitching the Design

Securing the First and Last Stitches. Don't knot the end of your yarn before you begin stitching. Instead, begin each length of yarn by coming up from the wrong side of the canvas and leaving a 1"-2" tail on the wrong side. Hold this tail against the canvas and work the first few stitches over the tail. When secure, clip the tail close to the stitched piece. Long tails can become tangled in future stitches or can show through to the right side of the canvas. After all the stitches of one color in an area are complete, end by running the needle under several stitches on the back. Trim the end close to the stitched piece.

Using Even Tension. Keep your stitching tension consistent, with each stitch lying flat and even. Pulling or yanking the yarn causes the tension to be too tight, and you will be able to see through your project. If the tension is too loose, the stitches won't lie flat. Most stitches tend to twist yarn. Drop your needle and let the yarn untwist occasionally.

Joining Pieces

Straight Edges. To join two or more pieces along a straight edge, place one piece on top of the other with right or wrong sides together. Make sure the edges are even, then overcast the pieces together through all layers.

Shaded Areas. Shaded areas usually mean that all the stitches in that area are used to join pieces of canvas. Do not work these stitches until the project instructions say you should.

Tacking. To tack pieces, run your needle under the backs of some stitches on one stitched piece to secure the yarn. Then run the needle through the canvas or under stitches on the piece to be tacked in place. This should securely attach pieces without tacking stitches showing.

Uneven Edges. When you join a diagonal edge to a straight edge, the holes will not line up exactly. Keep the pieces even and stitch through the holes as many times as necessary to completely cover the canvas.

Stitch Diagrams

*Unless otherwise indicated, bring needle up at **1** and all **odd** numbers and down at **2** and all **even** numbers.*

Backstitch

This stitch is worked over completed stitches to outline or define **(Fig. 2)**. It is sometimes worked over more than one thread. It can also be used to cover canvas **(Fig. 3)**.

Fig. 2

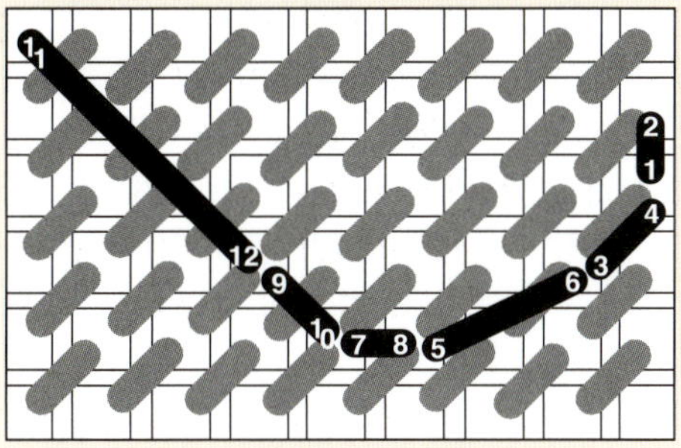

Fig. 3

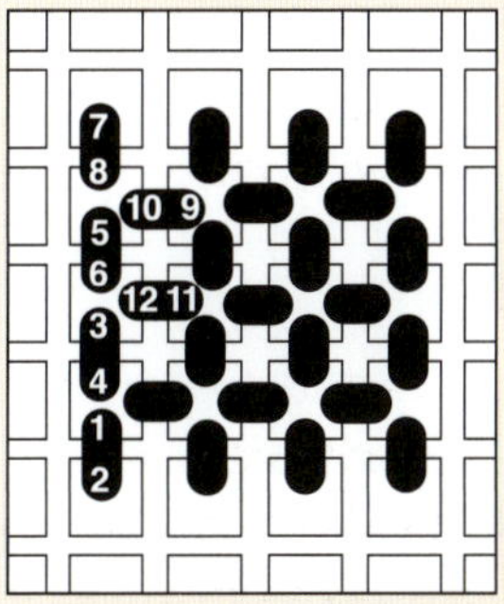

Boullion Knot

Come up at 1; go down at 2, leaving a loop yarn on top of canvas. The distance between 1 and 2 is the length of the knot. Come up at 1 **(Fig. 4)**. Wrap the loop around the needle as shown until the coil equals the distance between 1 and 2. Hold the coil in position while pulling the thread through **(Fig. 5)**. As the thread is pulled taut, the coil will fold back overe and lie on the canvas between 1 and 2. Secure the knot by going down at 2 **(Fig. 6)**.

Fig. 4

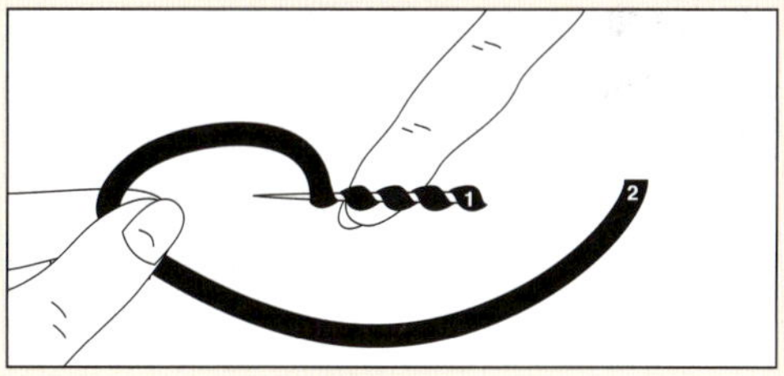

Fig. 5

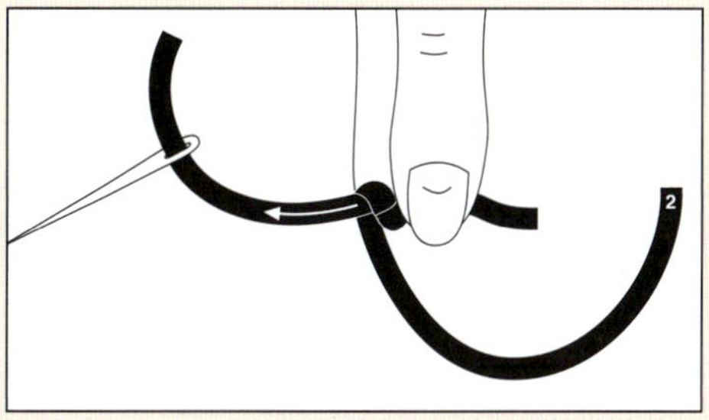

Fig. 6

Cross Stitch

This stitch is composed of two stitches **(Fig. 7)**. Cross the top leg of each stitch in the same direction. The number of intersections may vary according to the chart.

Fig. 7

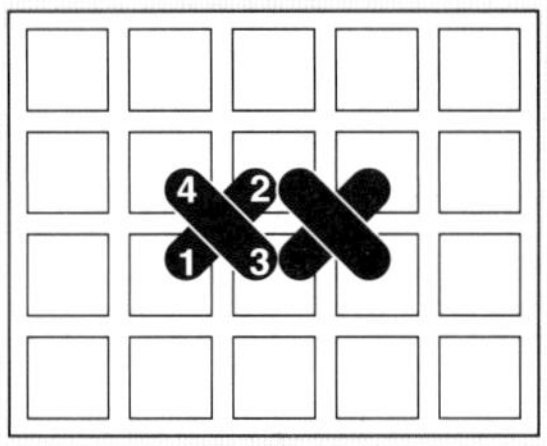

French Knot

Come up at 1. Wrap yarn once around needle. Insert the needle at 2 and pull it through the canvas, holding the yarn until it must be released **(Fig. 8)**.

Fig. 8

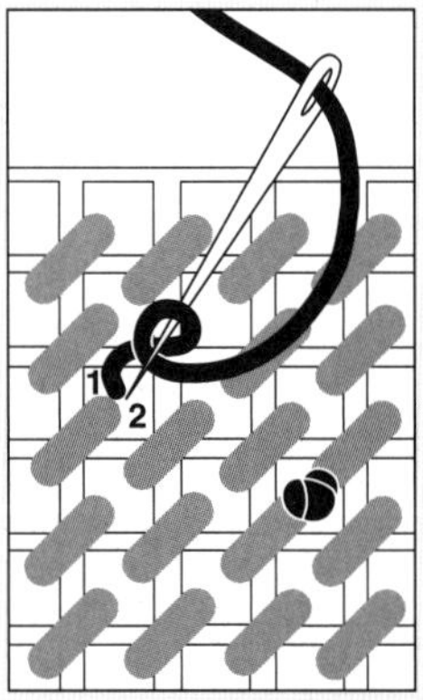

Fringe Stitch

Fold a length of yarn in half. Thread needle with loose ends of yarn. Bring needle up at 1, leaving a 1" loop on the back of the canvas. Bring needle around the edge of canvas and through loop **(Fig. 9)**. Pull to tighten loop **(Fig. 10)**. Trim fringe to desired length. A dot of glue on back of fringe will help keep stitch in place.

Fig. 9

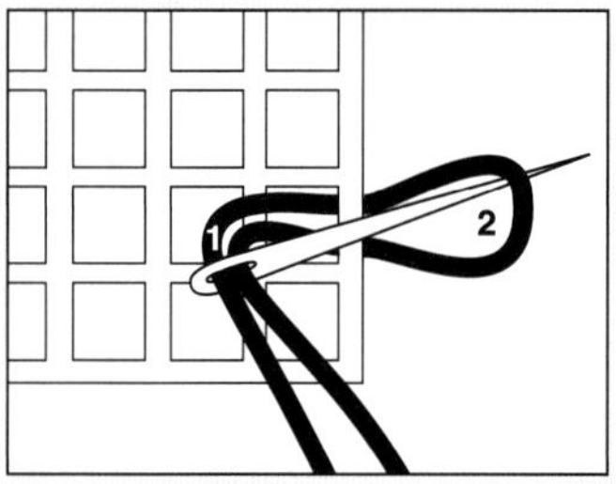

Fig. 10

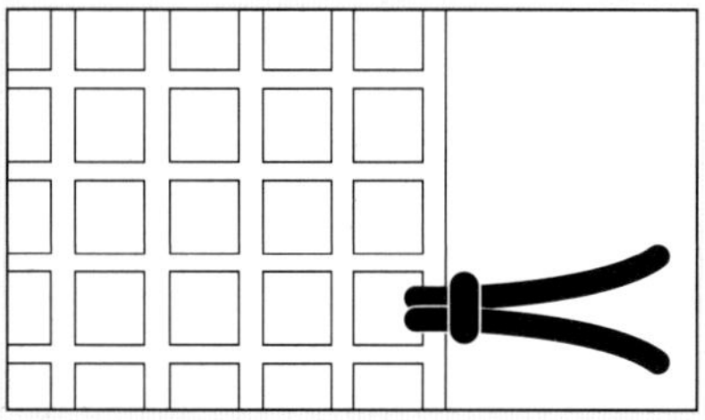

Gobelin Stitch

This straight stitch is worked over two or more threads or intersections **(Fig. 11)**. The number of threads or intersections may vary according to the chart.

Fig. 11

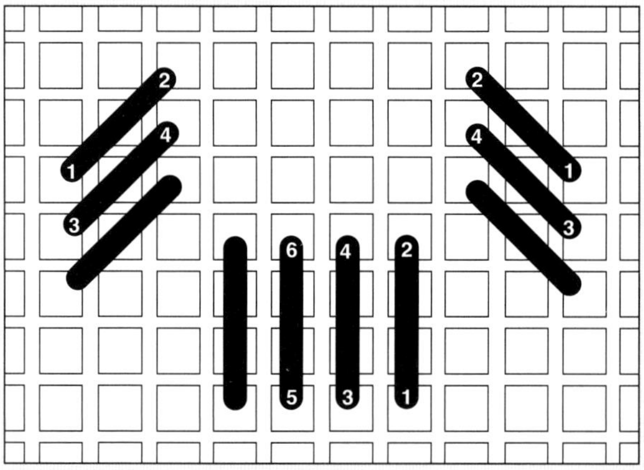

Overcast Stitch

This stitch covers the edge of canvas and joins pieces **(Fig. 12)**. It may be necessary to go through the same hole more than once to get even coverage on the edge, especially at the corners.

Fig. 12

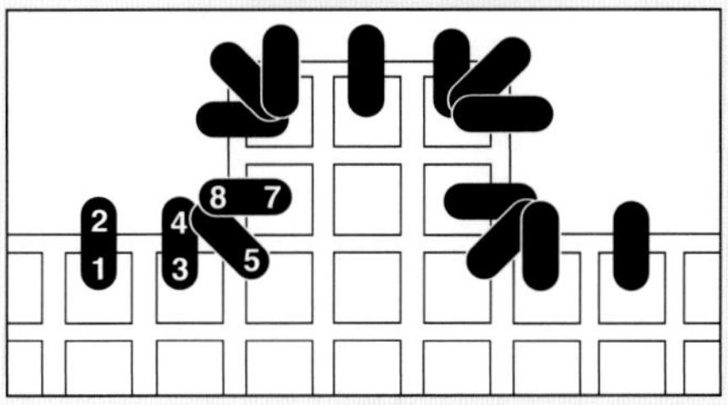

Tent Stitch

This stitch is worked in horizontal or vertical rows over one intersection **(Fig. 13)**. Refer to **Fig. 14** to work the reversed tent stitch.

Fig.13

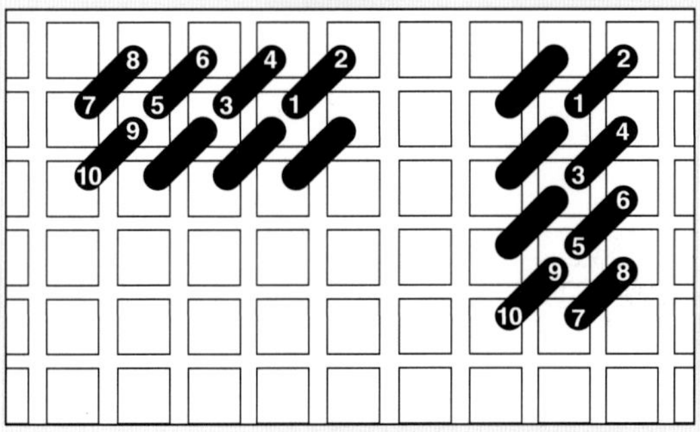

Fig. 14

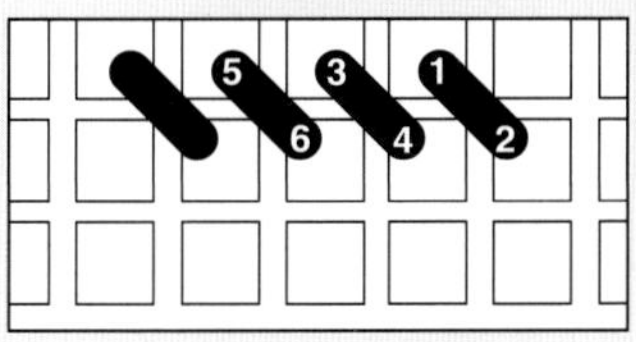

Turkey Loop Stitch

This stitch is composed of locked loops. Bring the needle up through hole and back down through same hole, forming a loop on top of the canvas. Make a locking stitch across the thread directly below or to either side of the loop as shown in **Fig. 15**.

Fig.15

Making A Pom-Pom

Referring to Diagram A, wrap 3 yards each of blue and red yarn around the cardboard. Remove cardboard from yarn circle. Referring to Diagram B, tie a 5" length of yarn around the center of the yarn circle. Clip loops of yarn circle; trim ends to shape.

Diagram A

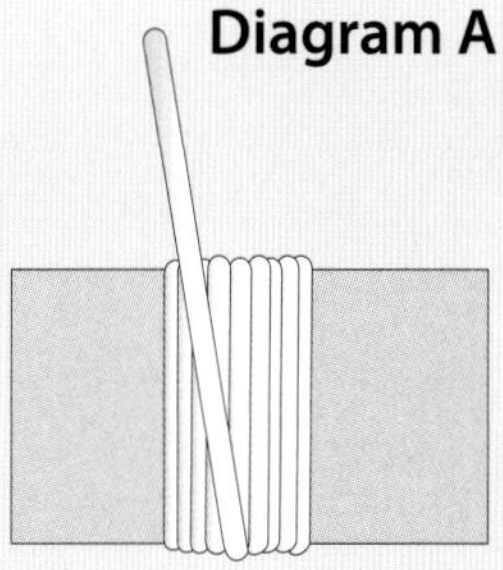

Diagram B

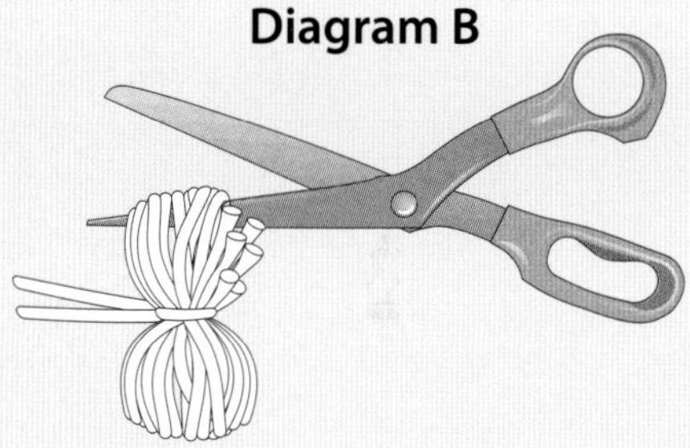

Library of Congress Control Number: 2019933131

Made in U.S.A.

We have made every effort to ensure that these instructions are accurate and complete. We cannot, however, be responsible for human error, typographical mistakes, or variations in individual work.